THE
AUGUST
COUP

MIKHAIL GORBACHEV

THE AUGUST COUP

The Truth and the Lessons

HarperCollins*Publishers*

HarperCollins*Publishers*,
77–85 Fulham Palace Road,
Hammersmith, London w6 8jb

9 8 7 6 5 4 3 2 1

A catalogue record for this book is
available from the British Library

ISBN 0 00 255044 X

Set in Linotron Garamond No. 3 by
Rowland Phototypesetting Ltd,
Bury St Edmunds, Suffolk

Printed in Great Britain by
Butler and Tanner Ltd,
Frome, Somerset

Contents

A Word to the Reader

The events that took place in the Soviet Union in August 1991 continue to be the subject of the keenest attention both in my country and in the world at large. Serious attempts are being made to analyse the causes and consequences of what took place. Unfortunately attempts of a different kind are also being made, aimed at turning those events into a topic for superficial speculation and for stirring up unworthy emotions and unhealthy attitudes. Irrespective of the intentions of the people who engage in that sort of thing, it does harm to the process of consolidating our society and reaching political agreement about what is now vitally necessary for our country.

I am, of course, also constantly thinking about what happened. I have already made some statements in public and I have said a great deal in conversations I have had in the past few weeks. I have now got everything together and would like to let readers have my assessment of the events. Further analysis, new facts, the course of events itself and, of course, the investigation into the charges of treason will provide material for a more thorough and well-founded understanding of all the circumstances and for arriving at the right conclusions. I am convinced, however, that fundamentally the judgements and opinions that I have set out here will not be upset.

M. Gorbachev
September 1991

THE
AUGUST
COUP

Like a Bolt from
the Blue?

The possibility of a *coup d'état* with the use of force and rumours
of the preparations being made for it had been circulating in
Soviet society for many months. Consequently the coup did
not come unexpectedly, like a bolt from the blue. In reply to
the straight question that was put to me more than once, I
had always said that a *coup d'état* in the present situation was
impossible, that it was doomed to fail, and that only madmen
could attempt it. In saying that I was far from wishing to
underestimate the danger of the hysteria which was being
whipped up by the right-wingers in the press and at meetings
of the Central Committee, of provocative speeches by certain
generals, and of the sabotage of many *perestroika* decisions by
the Party and state machinery at all levels.

Casting a retrospective glance back at the events of 19–21
August I have to say that the logic of the profound reforms
did not exclude such a turn of events. I recognized that events
could take on extremely dramatic forms. What was the basis
for such a supposition? Cardinal changes had affected the whole
social organism and the deeply rooted interests of all sections
of society.

Above all I have in mind the Party which ruled in the name
of the people without obtaining the authority to do so from
the people themselves. The changes affected the Army which
had been drawn into a process of far-reaching reforms as a

result of the policy of 'new thinking', the progress of disarmament and the acceptance of the doctrine of sufficient defence. The process of converting the military-industrial complex to civilian purposes has become a reality. It is advancing with difficulty, attended by many negative consequences. And yet the people employed in that sector of the economy constitute the best organized, intellectually strong and highly qualified section of society which also enjoys certain privileges.

Now add to that the ethnic aspects of the process of *perestroika*, the reform of the laws regarding property, intended to change the incentives for work, and the transition to a market economy. And much, much more. Everything has come together here at once.

The country had slid into a systemic crisis. The very logic of the development of society dictated the necessity for profound changes in the course of which a mass of contradictions emerged. The breakdown of the old system generated instability and chaos. There was in any case no way that reforms could be carried through easily in such a huge country, which had been for decades a totalitarian state with a monopoly over power and the complete domination of state ownership of property. The process of reform turned out to be very painful and had a serious effect on the life of the people.

In that situation the plotters undertook an attempt to return the country to totalitarianism. But the situation itself was also the result of the dilatory and inconsistent way in which our policies were put into practice, especially as regards the reform of the previous machinery of government. I have in mind the delay in abolishing the Party's monopoly of power and the structure of the Party bureaucracy, which have in many respects been handed down from the old regime, and the unjustified indulgence with regard to people who did not accept *perestroika* but preserved their loyalty to Stalinism and everything connected with it or who at best advocated post-Stalinism. Both at the twenty-eighth Party Congress and at the subsequent plenums of the Central Committee there was an exhausting battle between supporters of the democratic reforms and the people who strove in every way to block them. But the same thing was happening in the local Party committees. The old system was already undermined and disorganized, but it continued to hold back everything it could and obstructed the movement forward.

What happened at the time of the attempted *coup d'état* – a decisive clash between the forces of reaction and democracy – had to come about in some form or another. It marked the resolution of the contradictions that had accumulated.

Many people now say: did Gorbachev really not foresee it? Of course I did foresee the theoretical possibility of a sharp conflict between the forces of renewal and reaction. And I was not alone in that. But what conclusion was to be drawn from that?

From the very beginning of the crisis brought about by the radical transformation of our society I tried not to allow an explosive resolution of the contradictions to take place. I wanted to gain time by making tactical moves, so as to allow the democratic process to acquire sufficient stability to ease out the old ways and to strengthen people's attachment to the new values. In short, I wanted to bring the country to a stage where any such attempt to seize power would be doomed to failure. My principal objective was, despite all the difficulties, to continue along the course of reform and, however painful it might be, to keep the process moving on political and constitutional lines.

In the course of, roughly speaking, the last year and a half the confrontation between the forces of progress and reaction was intensifying. As from December or even the autumn of last year it assumed very acute forms. No attempt was even being made to disguise where some people stood. Repeated appeals were made for the adoption of emergency measures, and the plenums of the Central Committee turned into real battles. That was true of the April plenum in 1991 which came as a shock to the public. It was also true of the last plenum on the eve of which thirty-two of the seventy-two secretaries of the regional Party committees in the Russian Federation declared that Gorbachev should be called to account.

I recall the conversations I had with Felipe Gonzalez this summer in Moscow. I stated then, and he agreed with me, that an extremely sharp confrontation was taking place in our society between the old social and political structures and society itself, which had already undergone profound change. Those structures were doomed and had to be replaced. It was my constant desire to bring that about in a bloodless and democratic way. If only once in our country's history we could avoid bloodshed in a period of revolutionary change.

How else, after all, could the initiators of *perestroika* behave? What sort of democrats would they have been otherwise? As on the world stage as well, we kept firmly to a course that excluded the solution of problems by means of force. We sought to avert any attempt at a reactionary coup.

In a conversation I had on 11 September with the United States Secretary of State James Baker I heard him say: 'In the last few days George Bush and I have given a lot of thought, Mr President, to your policy and we have now understood your course of manœuvre and compromise. You wanted to gain time so as not to allow conservative forces to wreck the policy of reform.'

Yes, that is how it really was. The policy of compromise was essential to reduce tension at moments of serious danger.

That was the situation in September and December 1990 and again in the spring of 1991, when the shout went up: 'Down with the General Secretary! Down with the President!' I must note that the shouts came from various directions. We had to arrive at a course of action calculated to create the conditions for consolidating the reforms so that the public would understand them thoroughly and acquire the strength to defend them. It was precisely in such a tense situation that the President of the USSR and the leaders of nine republics gathered in Novo-Ogarevo and issued the now well-known joint declaration that has played an indispensable role. The Novo-Ogarevo process brought society to a new understanding of the need for accord in the country. I repeat: throughout these years my goal was to preserve and save the political course of *perestroika*. For that purpose I considered it essential to move forward more quickly to the conclusion of a Union treaty, to carry out radical economic transformations, and to reorganize the Party.

The draft of the Union treaty was ready for signature. On 20 August in the St George's Hall in the Kremlin delegations from six republics were due to sign it. As the country's President I was due to make a speech.

I had summoned a session of the Council of the Federation for 21 August – to discuss a plan for stepping up the reforms and the problems of food supplies, fuel, financial stabilization, and so on.

In short, we had to make a profound and decisive democratic breakthrough in the main directions of the reform process, to reach a new level on which there was already no room for people who did not wish or were not able to break away from the old centralized command way of thinking and acting. The plotters saw that time was fast running out for them, and so they chose that moment to put their plans into action. The attempted coup was a reaction to the Novo-Ogarevo process and to its most important result – the new treaty on the Union of Sovereign States.

Three Days on
Cape Foros

We went through a very difficult ordeal. The danger of the putsch lay in the fact that its organizers were at the very centre of the leadership, next to the President. The hardest thing that I suffered on the personal level was the treachery. That will haunt me to the end of my life.

The machinery of the coup was set in motion in Moscow. Everything had obviously been prepared in advance.

After lunch on 18 August, on Cape Foros in the Crimea, where I was on vacation, I went back to work on the text of the speech I was due to make at the signing of the Union treaty. I planned to fly to Moscow on 19 August. On the previous day I had talked with the Presidents of Russia and Kazakhstan, Yeltsin and Nazarbayev, about the forthcoming signing of the Treaty and the session of the Council of the Federation. Around midday on 18 August I talked with Vice-President Yanayev. Incidentally, he then thanked me for indicating to him the time of my arrival in Moscow and promised to meet me. Later I spoke with Velichko (Deputy Prime Minister), Volsky (President of the Scientific-Industrial Association), and Gurenko (First Secretary of the Central Committee of the Ukrainian Communist Party). Dementey (Chairman of Byelorussia's Supreme Soviet) did not answer my call — he was away somewhere. And at 4.30 p.m. I discussed my forthcoming speech over the telephone with my assistant Shakhnazarov. We now know that on 19 August it was announced that I was not capable of carrying out my functions. Of the people with whom I spoke on the 18th only two refuted the conspirators' announcement concerning my alleged illness, and even they did not do so at once but a day or two later.

At ten minutes to five in the afternoon of 18 August the head of my bodyguard informed me that a group of people had arrived and demanded to see me. I was not expecting anybody, had not invited anyone, and no one had informed me of anyone's possible arrival. The head of the bodyguard said that he also knew nothing about it. 'Then why did you let them in?' I asked. 'Plekhanov arrived with them,' he replied. (Plekhanov was head of the department in charge of personal protection in the State Security Committee). Otherwise the guards would not have allowed them to approach the President. Those are the rules, strict but essential.

My first wish was to establish who had sent the people to me. I was actually working in my office at the time. Since the whole communication system was with me – the government line, the normal line, the strategic and the satellite communications – I picked up a receiver of one of the telephones – it was dead. I picked up a second receiver, then a third, a fourth and a fifth – they were all dead. Then I picked up the internal telephone – it had been cut off. Yet twenty minutes previously the communication system had been working. The conspirators had apparently decided in advance that they would not succeed in coming to terms with me and had prepared the alternative of isolating me.

I realized that for me this mission would not be the kind I was accustomed to dealing with. First of all I told my wife and then my daughter and son-in-law what had happened. It was clear to me that it was something very serious. I did not exclude an attempt at blackmail or arrest or something else.

In fact anything might happen. 'You must know,' I told Raisa Maksimovna, Irina and Anatoli, 'that I will not give in to any kind of blackmail, nor to any threats or pressure and will not retreat from the positions I have taken up.'

But one could not exclude the possibility that this might be followed by the most severe measures also with regard to members of my family.

The whole family agreed that it was up to me to decide and that they were ready to share with me to the end whatever was ahead. That was the end of our consultation.

I went off to invite the visitors in, but they had already come up to my office without being asked – an unheard-of lack of respect. The group consisted of Boldin, the man in charge of the President's staff, Shenin, a member of the Politburo and a secretary of the Central Committee, Baklanov, my deputy on the Defence Council and a former secretary of the Central Committee. The fourth man with them was Varennikov, General of the Army and a person very remote from me but who was nevertheless the man who later travelled to the Ukraine and presented Kravchuk, Chairman of the Ukranian Supreme Soviet, with an ultimatum. Plekhanov was also with them, but I ordered him out of my office.

At the very beginning of this encounter I put the question: 'Before continuing our conversation I want to ask you who sent you?' The reply was: 'The Committee.'

Then the following dialogue took place:

'What committee?"

'Well, the Committee set up to deal with the emergency situation in the country.'

'Who set it up? I didn't create it and the Supreme Soviet didn't create it. Who created it?'

What the visitors had to say was that people had already got together and now needed a decree from the President.

They put the situation facing me like this: either you issue the decree and remain here or you hand over your powers to the Vice-President. Baklanov said that Yeltsin had been arrested. Then he corrected himself: he would be arrested on the way.

'What are the grounds for putting the question in this way?'

'The situation the country is in – it is heading for catastrophe, steps must be taken, a state of emergency is needed – other measures won't save us, we must no longer let ourselves be deluded . . .' And so on.

My reply consisted of telling them that I knew no less than they did the political, economic and social situation in the country, the state people were in, how they lived and the heavy burdens they were now bearing. We needed to do more quickly all that was necessary to improve the standard of living. But I was a determined opponent – not just for political and moral reasons – of ways of solving problems which had always led in the past to the deaths of hundreds, thousands and millions of people. We must reject that course for ever. Otherwise everything we had started to do would be betrayed and buried and we would set out again on another bloody course. If they had a different view, I said, then let us raise these questions in the Supreme Soviet, have them discussed in the Congress of People's Deputies and seek solutions. My position was in any case well known to them: I had stated it in the Supreme Soviet and fought for it at meetings of the Central Committee and the Politburo. I rejected their ultimatum.

I had succeeded more than once in recent years in checking or averting a dangerous turn of events. And this time I again thought that these people would understand and change their minds. So I said: 'You and the people who sent you are irresponsible. You will destroy yourselves, but that's your business and to hell with you. But you will also destroy the country and everything we have already done. Tell that to the committee that sent you.

'We are now about to sign the Union treaty. Together with the republics major decisions have been prepared with regard to food supplies and fuel and financial problems in order to stabilize as quickly as possible the political and economic situation, to speed up the transition to a market economy and to give people greater opportunities to develop in every way. We were on the way to reaching agreement. Of course, we do not have enough agreement yet: we have not yet rid ourselves of suspicion on both sides. It is still there in relations between the republics and the centre and in relations between political and social movements. But the only way is to seek agreement. It has emerged and we have begun to move ahead. Only people bent on committing suicide could now propose to introduce a state of emergency in the country. I will not have anything to do with it.'

It was at that moment that Varennikov demanded: 'Give in your resignation.' I rejected the general's insolent demand, saying: 'You'll get neither one thing nor the other out of me – tell that to all the people who sent you here.

'Actually, there is a possibility of meeting with many republican leaders and discussing these questions. On 20 August we are signing the new Union treaty. On 21 August there is to be a session of the Council of the Federation. We shall be discussing matters we couldn't agree on in the Cabinet of Ministers. We must reach some decisions. But not the way you want to do it.

'So tomorrow you will declare a state of emergency. What then? Can you plan for at least one day ahead, four steps further – what next? The country will reject these measures, it will not support them. You want to exploit the difficulties, the fact that the people are tired, you think that they are already prepared to support any dictator . . .'

Incidentally, during the preceding days I had actually been working with my assistant Chernyayev on a major article. It dealt with the situation in the country and the possible ways it might evolve. And one of the scenarios considered was in fact the introduction of a state of emergency. And now the characters from it had turned up here. My reasoning about that scenario consisted in saying that it would be a disaster for our society and a dead end, that it would turn the country back and bury everything we now have . . .

'I propose that we call a meeting of the Supreme Soviet and the Congress, and resolve everything there. You are worried about the present situation? So are all of us. You believe there is need for urgent measures. I am of the same opinion. So let's get together and take some decisions. I am prepared to agree to the convening of the Congress of People's Deputies and the Supreme Soviet since some of the country's leaders have doubts. Let's get together, let's discuss things. The Deputies know what is going on in their localities. Let us take steps. I shall defend three main directions of policy: the path of seeking accord, the path of extending the reforms, and cooperation with the West. Especially since other nations do wish to collaborate with us now at this decisive stage.'

But it was like talking to deaf and dumb people. The machine had been set in motion – that was now clear. I said: 'That's it, then. There can be no more talk. Report back that I am categorically opposed to your plans and that you will be defeated. But I am fearful for our people and for what we have achieved in recent years.'

The one who behaved in the crudest manner was Varennikov. At one point I said to him: 'I don't remember your name

(I did remember, of course!) – oh, yes, Valentin Ivanovich, is it? – so just listen, Valentin Ivanovich. The people are not a battalion of soldiers to whom you can issue the command "right turn" or "left turn, march" and they will all do as you tell them. It won't be like that. Just mark my words.' And at the end of the conversation, using the strongest language that the Russians always use in such circumstances, I told them where to go. And that was the end of it.

In the course of the conversation I repeated several times: 'Think again – this affair will end in a civil war and a great deal of bloodshed. You will have to answer for it. You are adventurers and criminals. Still, nothing will come of your plans. The people are no longer ready to put up with your dictatorship or with the loss of everything we have gained in recent years.'

Once they had received my categorical rejection of their ultimatum everything then followed the logic of the conflict. The plotters isolated me completely from the outside world, both from the sea and the land, creating what was essentially psychological pressure. I was totally isolated. Later in Moscow I learned that a frontier unit and a group of frontier protection ships had been put under the direct command of Plekhanov and Generalov (his deputy) for this purpose. I was left with the thirty-two men of my bodyguard. I soon got to know their position. They had decided to stand firm and protect me to the end and divided the entire place into areas of responsibility.

It was not difficult to foresee the logic of the plotters' further actions: on the basis of a lie they would seize power and use it for their own ends. Confirmation of this was the press conference organized on 19 August by the so-called State Committee for the Emergency. They announced that, on account of the state of my health, I was not capable of carrying out the functions of President. Moreover, they promised to produce a medical certificate in the near future. I took it that that meant that if the facts did not correspond with their statements, that is, if the President's condition differed from what they said, they would have by whatever means to reduce him to such a condition so that he really was broken physically and psychologically.

The comrades in my bodyguard understood this too. It was decided that we should refuse to accept the food that was brought in every day from outside and live off what supplies we had and what was being provided in the bodyguards' dining room. Vigilance had to be increased in every respect.

What made the greatest impression on me, and I believe, on others, was not what the plotters said at the press conference but their pitiful appearance. I remained totally composed, although I was shaken to the very depths and angry at those people's political blindness and criminal lack of a sense of responsibility. I was sure, quite convinced that the whole business could not continue for long – they would not get away with it.

Already in the afternoon of 19 August I handed over a demand for the immediate restoration of communications and for a plane to be sent for me to fly to Moscow. There was no reply.

Following the press conference I decided immediately to record myself on a video tape. We made four recordings and the children, Irina and Anatoli, cut the film into four parts and we started to look for reliable channels through which we could somehow get the films out. My doctor wrote out several copies of his opinion, so that everyone should know the true state of the President's health. I dictated to Chernyayev the four points constituting my demands. After it had been typed out I added the opening sentence in longhand and my signature, so that it should be clear that it had been written by me personally. Here is the text:

I bring to the attention of the Congress of People's Deputies and the USSR Supreme Soviet the following

DECLARATION

1. G.I. Yanayev's assumption of the duties of President on the pretext that I am ill and unable to carry out my responsibilities is an attempt to deceive the people and thus cannot be described as anything but a *coup d'état*.

2. That means that all subsequent acts are also illegal and unlawful.

Neither the President nor the Congress of People's Deputies has given Yanayev such authority.

3. Please convey to comrade Lukyanov my demand for the urgent summoning of the Supreme Soviet of the USSR and the Congress of People's Deputies to consider the situation that has arisen.

Because they and only they, having considered the situation, have the right to decide the question of the measures to be taken by the government and the means of putting them into practice.

4. I demand the immediate suspension of the activity of the State Committee for the Emergency until the above decisions have been taken by the Supreme Soviet or the Congress of People's Deputies of the USSR.

The continuation of these actions and the further escalation of measures taken by the State Committee for the Emergency can turn out to be a tragedy for all the peoples, further aggravate the situation and even completely wreck the joint work that the Centre and the

republics have begun in order to find a way out of the
crisis.

Президент СССР

М. Горбачёв

President of the USSR
M. Gorbachev

Крым,
20. VIII. 1991 года.

The Crimea
20.8.1991

I demanded a reply. This time they told me to wait, there
would be one. But there was nothing. That was the situation.

Every day, morning and evening, I produced and handed
over my demands that communication should be restored and
that a plane should be sent immediately so that I could fly to
Moscow and my place of work. After the press conference
given by Yanayev and company I added to those demands that
a denial should be published admitting the falsity of the report
about the state of my health – a report issued by such very
healthy people whose hands trembled during their press conference.

Later, in Moscow, two doctors brought me a note in which
they described what had been demanded of them: Gorbachev
was allegedly under threat of arrest and had to be saved; they
were to 'provide a stronger diagnosis' to say that Gorbachev
was gravely ill. And they demanded that it should be done
before 4 p.m. on the 19th, before the notorious press confer-

ence, presumably so that they could announce it there. Moreover it was written that on the 16th there had been a breakdown of the blood circulation in the brain, that the President's condition was very serious, that he was bedridden, unable to understand what was going on around him, and so on. This in spite of the fact that on 16, 17 and 18 August I had conducted intensive talks concerning some important events that were coming up – the signing of the Union treaty and the session of the Council of the Federation.

The most difficult aspect of the situation was the lack of information. Everything was cut off except the television on which statements by the State Committee for the Emergency alternated with feature films and orchestral concerts. But the security officers from the bodyguard, very smart boys, found some old radio receivers in the service areas, fixed up aerials and started to pick up foreign broadcasts. The best reception was from the BBC and Radio Liberty. Later we managed to pick up the Voice of America. My son-in-law Anatoli managed to listen to a Western station on his pocket Sony. We started to collect and analyse information and assess the way the situation was developing.

What happened to us in the course of those days is deserving of serious analysis. But I reject any speculation about the position taken up by the President. The President's position was one of principle, which upset the plotters' cards and opened up the possibility that we, uniting our efforts from all sides, could inflict defeat on them.

The attempt to blackmail the President, to make him issue a decree introducing the state of emergency, to hand over his authority and abandon his post – all this failed.

I reject categorically any suggestion hinting that the President was not equal to the situation or that he was concerned with saving his own skin.

The forces that have been defeated will try to think up all kinds of things. They will produce the crudest inventions, try to cast suspicion on the President and the democratic forces, and to compromise them.

Here is one story that is going round: It suggests that I knew in advance about the putsch, and is based on a reference to the interview given by Lukyanov on 19 August. The investigation will reveal everything, including the value to be attached to the rumour being put about suggesting that Gorbachev's communications were not cut off, but that he kept out of the way so as to sit it out and then to arrive 'ready to serve'. A 'no-lose' situation, so to speak. If the coup succeeded, then the President, having given them the chance, would win out. If the coup failed, he would again be right. Similar lies are being spread from various sides. Incidentally, on 18 August, when he was trying to get me to agree to order a state of emergency or hand over to Yanayev, Baklanov argued in the same spirit as the present character assassins. Appealing to me to support the Committee, he said: 'You take a rest and while you are away we'll do the "dirty work"(*sic*) and you will return to Moscow.' A strange coincidence, is it not? But if those three days failed to unsettle me it certainly won't happen now.

Raisa Maksimovna behaved courageously, as did all the members of the family, although they understood what was at stake. I am proud of my family. On 18 August I was still hoping that the people in Moscow, having heard a report about the meeting with me, would stop and think again. The morning announcements (we had managed to switch the television on – how we did it I have described above – on 19 August) upset my expectations, my hope that the plotters would come to their senses.

Along with the family and Chernyayev I decided, despite all the possible 'accidents' there might be, to make myself visible – let everybody see that the President was alive and well and in his normal condition. Let them compare and draw their own conclusions.

At the moment when the BBC announced that a group of plotters were on their way apparently for the purpose of showing the Russian delegation and the Soviet people and the public at large the state Gorbachev was in we all took it to mean that some treachery had been thought up. It was at that moment that Raisa Maksimovna suffered a serious attack of pain from which she took some time to recover. I have already spoken about it – it was fortunate that we were at her side.

Anastasia, my granddaughter, was the one who bore up best . . . She understood nothing, just ran around and demanded to be taken down to the sea. And they had to take her. But later the bodyguard insisted that we should stop that too because anything could happen. Raisa Maksimovna and our daughter Irina were those who suffered the most.

Defeat of the Plotters

The three days in August were a real watershed. I sometimes say that what happened before the coup was, so to speak, before the new era, and after it was the beginning of a new epoch.

Let me say again that, to a certain extent, I did foresee that something of the kind might take place, that there were difficult times ahead. It might have happened even in the autumn of last year. My main task consisted in sustaining the policy of radical reform of society, and in protecting that most complicated process from overreaching itself or going right off the rails. All the tactical moves and actions were subordinated to that end.

If the *coup d'état* had happened a year and a half or two years earlier it might, presumably, have succeeded. But now society was completely changed. The people who, five years previously, had been thirteen to fifteen years old were now eighteen or twenty. They had grown up in a different atmosphere. And they had become the most courageous defenders of democracy.

The whole of society had changed, including the Army that was part of it. Officers and privates refused to go against their own people despite the threat of court martial. The forces of law and order and even the special commando troops behaved similarly. That was where the plotters went wrong: they did not realize that society was now not at all what it had been a few years back.

It had breathed the air of freedom and no one could now take that away from it. Certainly the people want the rule of law and stability, but not by means of dictatorship and not by states of emergency. The people were certainly tired of waiting for the standard of living to improve. But the people wanted a way out of the crisis to be found within the framework of democracy and not at the expense of freedom and human rights, not through the use of force.

The plotters totally failed to understand the new relations between the USSR and its partners in the West. They ignored the tremendous fundamental changes in the international situation of our state, especially in our relations with the peoples of the USA and Europe. Perhaps there were at the outset some hesitations in the assessment of the coup, but the overwhelming majority of the governments very soon gave a firm 'no' to the plotters and refused to collaborate with them in any way.

The interaction of these two factors – the democratic achievements of *perestroika* and the new relationship with the world outside – predetermined the plotters' defeat.

I was always convinced – even when they presented me with the ultimatum to hand over my powers to the Vice-President or to announce my resignation 'to save our Fatherland' – that their wild scheme would not succeed and that they would be defeated. They were pushing the country and the people into a catastrophe. And they will have to answer for it.

Their plans were far-reaching: first of all, to strike at the most advanced democratic forces that have assumed responsibility for the democratic transformation of the country and would keep to their course despite all the reversals and difficulties. That was the main plan. An element in it was to blackmail the President of the USSR and announce that the

President of Russia was arrested. In other words, they counted on striking a blow, isolating me if I didn't agree to collaborate with the forces of reaction and isolating the President of the Russian Federation. The investigation and court proceedings will reveal whether it was to be only a case of isolating us.

But the democratic forces showed that, once they were united and acting together, they could defend the policy of extending the reforms and transformations, the path to a new society.

The most difficult day was 19 August and the night from the 20th to the 21st, although it was already apparent on 20 August that the plotters were not succeeding. Their plans had been upset by the stand taken by the President of the USSR and the Russian leadership. In the republics too things began to change, although initially some of them hesitated.

A tremendous part was played by the battle organized against the plotters by Boris Yeltsin. He took up a brave position and acted decisively, taking all the responsibility on himself. In those extraordinary circumstances it was justified and when I returned to Moscow I confirmed the decrees he had issued at the time of the putsch. I believe that in that situation the Russian leaders acted in the highest interests. What they did was dictated by the situation. Without the firm position they adopted events might have acquired a more dramatic character.

At the same time I must mention the position of principle and courage taken up by the people of Moscow, Leningrad and many of the regions of Russia. The position of the presidents and parliaments of the majority of the republics and local Soviets was of great significance in defeating the conspiracy. They succeeded in taking a firm stand in defence of the rule of law and their sovereign rights. At that difficult time the majority of journalists and the media made no mistake in choosing where and with whom to be: they did not take fright or behave as cowards or curry favour with the usurpers. Efforts on the part of the plotters to give the impression that the whole country supported them were seen to be pathetic and laughable.

Thus the Novo-Ogarevo process had borne fruit. We had created it at the right time and it made a difference in a dramatic situation.

The conspirators tried to do the most frightful thing: to turn the Army against its own people. But this didn't work for them either. Many commanders, officers and most soldiers, whole units and other formations refused to carry out their orders. They remained true to their oath and stood side by side with the brave defenders of democracy.

Incidentally, when we come to talk about generals, let us not forget that General Shaposhnikov did not join the conspirators. Yet, after all, it would have needed no more than three planes and there would have been nothing but ruins left of the 'White House' (the Supreme Soviet of the Russian Federation) and even of the Kremlin. The commander of the Leningrad military district, Samsonov, after speaking with the mayor of the city said: you can rest assured that there will be no troops in Leningrad. I was told that by Anatoli Sobchak, the Mayor.

The Army showed that it is already a different army: as a result of very difficult and painful changes brought about by *perestroika* a new army is being born in our country. And we must give it its due. If it were not the case it would have been very simple for the plotters to carry out their plans.

There is now a lot of talk questioning the intellectual abilities of the participants in the *coup d'état*. To agree with it would mean committing a great over-simplification. By no means. Then what was their problem? I think everything springs from their political stand. They did not accept *perestroika* and democratic transformations and took criminal steps counting primarily on people's discontent.

The plotters embarked on a monstrous deception in announcing that the President was seriously ill and incapable of performing his duties. The most frightful aspect of this was the treachery. Take the case of Lukyanov, Chairman of the Supreme Soviet. He came up to me in a corridor after one of the meetings of the Supreme Soviet. We had not spoken since he had turned up in Foros on the 21st. What's more, I had no desire to talk to him. I had relied on Lukyanov, reckoning that he would not betray our cause or me. For forty years, from our student days, we had enjoyed comradely relations. His behaviour could not be explained by cowardice, nor by lack of intellect – that was out of the question in his case, so it meant that it was a case of pure calculation. The official investigation will clarify the matter.

Everybody can now see that, in the course of those six years, with such difficulty and in such extraordinary and complex conditions, we had not been seeking the path ahead in vain. Society had acquired a great deal. It had acquired freedom. The country rejected the attempt to drive it on to the path of bloodshed. I think it would be difficult to conceive of a better argument or a more authoritative plebiscite.

In all the conversations I had in the first hours and days after returning to Moscow – with George Bush, François Mitterrand, Helmut Kohl, John Major, Giulio Andreotti, Brian Mulroney, Bob Hawke, Toshiki Kaifu, Hosni Mubarak and other heads of states and governments – nobody voiced approval of the plotters. Only Gaddafi and Saddam Hussein supported them.

When it became clear what an uncompromising position had been taken by Russia, its leaders, other republics and the majority of the country's population, and when it became evident that the Army did not support the plotters, the self-styled Committee took panic and began to seek a way out.

So around five o'clock in the evening of 21 August there in the south I was informed that a group of plotters had arrived in the Crimea in the presidential aircraft. I did not know at that point that there had been a talk between the Russian leaders and the Committee for the Emergency in which the latter had invited Boris Yeltsin to fly to the Crimea with them so that he could be convinced of the state of Gorbachev's health. When the plotters turned up at the dacha I gave orders that they should be arrested, and I issued my demand that I would not speak to any of them until the government telephone line was reconnected. They replied through the guard that it would take a long time. I instructed that they should be told: never mind, I'll wait.

The telephone was reconnected. The operators told me that Kryuchkov, Chairman of the KGB, wanted to talk to me. I replied: let him wait. Then I immediately called Boris Yeltsin, Nazarbayev, Kravchuk, Dementey and Karimov, the President of Uzbekistan. Then I called General Moiseyev and informed him that I was removing Defence Minister Yazov from his functions and transferring them provisionally to him, Moiseyev, and demanded that all troops should be returned to their quarters. I instructed the head of the government communications network to cut off the telephones of all the plotters. Some time later he reported that my instructions had been carried out. I gave orders to the commandant of the Kremlin not to let any of the supporters of the Committee out of the Kremlin. I instructed Moiseyev and Panyukov (Minister of Civil Aviation) to arrange for the plane carrying the Russian delegation headed by Vice-President Rutskoi to land on the military aerodrome at Belbek, near Foros. From Foros I also had a conversation with President Bush.

I ought to have telephoned my mother. But I was unable to do it. I still regret that. But as soon as we got to Moscow Raisa Maksimovna and I called and talked to both our mothers – Maria Panteleyevna and Alexandra Petrovna.

I was informed that Ivashko (Deputy General Secretary of the Party Central Committee) and Lukyanov were begging insistently to be received: they asserted that they were not involved with the plotters. I received them later. Bakatin, Primakov (Members of the USSR Security Council) and Chernyayev took part in the conversation. The others – Kryuchkov, Baklanov and Yazov – I did not receive. I did not even set eyes on them. We split them up in different aircraft and took them to Moscow where Yazov and Kryuchkov were arrested as they left the aircraft and held in isolation. Baklanov (who had parliamentary immunity) was arrested after the agreement of the Supreme Soviet had been obtained.

The attempt to seize power had been defeated. But there had been bloodshed. Some defenders of freedom lost their lives. I offer my deepest condolences to their families, their relations and near ones, their friends and colleagues. Their names should be inscribed on memorials at the places where they perished. They will remain in our hearts.

I want to reaffirm what I said in those days: punitive measures and legal responsibility for the coup must apply to its organizers and those who participated directly in it.

The democrats, those who inflicted defeat on the plotters, must do everything they can so that people should not get the idea that there is now going to be a search for 'the fall guys' or any sort of 'witch-hunt' aiming to extend responsibility. It is the organizers and those guilty of the conspiracy who should be punished. I have appealed to all prosecutors, the ministries of internal affairs of the Soviet Union and of the republics and the KGB to be governed only by that approach. That is the opinion of the leaders of the republics with whom I have spoken on this matter.

I have called the August events a watershed. After I returned from the Crimea and after the 'blockade' I was struck by the state our society was in. The country was in a state of shock and confusion. Immediately after the collapse of the attempt to seize power and as a reaction to it there developed a powerful process of disintegration of the country. There followed a series of demonstrative moves and declarations of independence. It was a sort of self-defence on the part of the republics in reply to the putsch.

There was increasing alarm due to the growing threat that the Soviet Union would fall apart. We must assess realistically the reaction to the coup in the country. We must not under-estimate or fail to take account of the fact that there were forces that were in sympathy with the plotters or took up a neutral position. The reactionary forces have been deprived of leadership, but the situation remains complex. It has not become any easier, though tremendous new possibilities have been opened up for continuing democratic reforms.

What took place was a very painful lesson for me personally. In the days and weeks that have passed I have reconsidered and reassessed a great deal. I have drawn my conclusions from the tragedy that has happened to us. It was said that I arrived back to a different country. I agree. I can add that the man who returned from the Crimea to a different country now looks at everything – the past, the present and the future – with different eyes. In any case I shall not permit any hesitation or any temporizing in carrying out reforms so long as I remain President. And henceforward there will be no compromise with those with whom it is not right to seek agreement.

But today, maybe more than yesterday, I want everything that we do to take place within the framework of democracy and without bloodshed.

Anyway, we now had to act. Much was still not clear. It was the beginning of a new era.

The Lessons of the Coup

Every time I try to analyse what happened and to get to the bottom of it I try to understand what prompted people to engage in treachery. I think it is not just a question of my mistakes in the selection of people. After all, there were some among them whom I knew and had worked with for many years. That means that *perestroika* had exposed a really fundamental difference of views concerning what we ought ultimately to arrive at. These people turned out to be incapable of understanding or accepting where *perestroika* was leading us.

The August events confirmed the irreversibility of the changes to which democratization and *glasnost* had brought us. A real breakthrough to a new way of life had taken place. Huge masses of people had become aware of themselves as citizens for whom, despite all the hardships of daily life, freedom had become of the highest value.

Another reason why the coup did not succeed was that the world around us condemned it and spoke in defence of democracy in our country, regarding it as a part of the whole democratic world. It was a natural position to adopt: thanks to the 'new thinking' and the foreign policy based on it, the Soviet Union had ceased to be an antagonist in that world. The success of *perestroika* is now seen as an essential condition for the security and progress of the whole of mankind.

We should make our judgements about everything soberly,

be merciless in our analysis, take a realistic view of things, and recognize that there were conditions with which the plotters linked their plans. Mistakes had been made in the social and economic sphere and in what concerned the dismantling of the old structures. Moreover, the Novo-Ogarevo process should have been started earlier.

The plotters counted on widespread discontent among the people because of the weakening of order in the country and the inability of the authorities to guarantee the security of people and property. They intended to exploit the concern in society due to the dangers resulting from inter-ethnic conflicts and the threat that the country would disintegrate.

They also counted on the fact that the democratic forces had not become properly aware of the vital necessity for joint action and collaboration. The democrats acted in an uncoordinated way, even entering into political battles with each other. We, people who were essentially committed to the same ends, were being divided and sometimes we were even led to the opposite sides of the political barricades. I have said more than once that when various groups among those who support democracy come into conflict and engage in political battles with each other, that is the best possible gift to the people who are against the policy of reforms. It was the result of the democrats' insufficient discernment and sense of responsibility for the common cause. This criticism also applies to me in full measure.

It is true that the conspirators did not succeed in carrying through to the end their criminal plan to hurl the Army against the population. The Army turned out to be with the people.

But nevertheless it turned out to be possible to bring out on to the streets a huge number of troops, tanks and other armoured equipment without any agreement on the part of the country's supreme legislative body. That is an obvious fact, and it means that there is something wrong in our machinery of government.

The obviously necessary reorganization of the Committee of State Security (KGB) had not been carried out. Of course, the employees of the security service defend the interests of the state by gathering intelligence and conducting counter-intelligence. That is what the Committee has to do. However, along with that, even in conditions of profound democratic transformations, it had still preserved as part of its organization what are essentially the functions of political investigation and ideological struggle.

The conspirators would not have been able to carry out their plans if the Supreme Soviet of the USSR and its Chairman had stood firmly and resolutely in their way. The events demanded the immediate summoning of the Supreme Soviet. Russia did so promptly and that played a tremendous part in resisting the coup. But the Supreme Soviet of the USSR failed to exercise its constitutional powers.

Where was its Presidium? Where were the Deputies themselves? Why did they not rush immediately to the capital? When such a situation arises, it would seem that, without any telegrams, summonses or announcements, all of them should be in the capital, where the supreme organ of power operates.

For if the Supreme Soviet had met on 19 August the coup could have been halted at the very beginning. That means we must devise a constitutional machinery that would exclude a repetition of what happened. However authoritative the people may be who head the Supreme Soviet, there must be a mechanism to ensure, in critical and fateful situations in the country, the immediate activation of the Supreme Soviet, our highest legislative body, into the defence of the rule of law, legal order and citizens' rights.

For the fact that the machinery of the Supreme Soviet of the USSR did not work, that many members of the Cabinet of Ministers were found to be shamelessly helpless and cowardly in the face of the conspiracy, that the three organizations disposing of armed force were headed by people capable of joining in a *coup d'état*, for that I as President bear a great, more precisely the greater part of responsibility.

We must draw all the lessons from what happened, and not just on the moral-political level. We must devise and establish a reliable system of constitutional and public control over the activity of the armed forces and the organs of law and order. The Committee of State Security (KGB) must be reorganized without delay.

A great deal is already being done, decided and changed in this field.

The main lesson for us arising from the events of August is that we must speed up the process of democratic reform.

Above all, we must remove all the obstacles and impediments that were created by the old structures and their people on the path to a market economy, offer complete freedom to business, get rid of monopolies and methods involving compulsion and dictation from above, and speed up the creation of the main institutions of a market economy.

With this aim in view I have supported a proposal to create a Council of entrepreneurs attached to the office of the President of the country. It has already produced its first plans aimed at encouraging entrepreneurial activity in all sectors of the economy.

We must resolutely support anything that will give the land reform a second breath. There is land, and all the obstacles ought to be removed that hinder its being offered to anyone who wants to cultivate it. The support of the state is essential here. All these problems must be resolved this autumn and winter. It is obvious that in this case too we must make use of the initiative of the public.

We cannot put off any longer the fundamental reform of our credit and financial policy. There must be a drastic reduction in budgetary expenditure and of the budgetary deficit, and the normalization of the money in circulation.

We need a fundamental reform of all our foreign economic relations including procedures involving foreign currency, the effective use of credits and other economic aid, and the implementation of major projects.

We must stop making unfounded promises and unrealistic plans, and abandon economic populism. Let us concentrate attention on the main questions concerning the social protection of the working people at a time of transition to a market economy: maintenance of the standard of living of the people, especially those with low incomes, and providing employment and housing.

There is no time to lose. If we don't let it be felt that we are taking action we shall lose people's trust. For by suppressing the putsch we have, I repeat, only struck the head of the dragon. The forces of reaction are still there and they are very real. They are taking steps to consolidate their positions, counting on our inactivity and inertia.

Finally, all of us who have defeated the conspiracy and who stood firm in the way of criminal plans should not to any degree allow our emotions and desires to run high or use the same methods that the conspirators resorted to. There is such a danger. But if it became a reality we would lose everything we gained as a result of defeating the coup.

Now we must be very attentive, keep our nerve, and not yield to provocation. There is much difficult work ahead. Above all we must do everything we can to give people an improvement of their life. That is now the top priority.

What we have been through recently was a drama that pushed all the problems and contradictions to the limit. But, on the other hand, these events, like flood waters in spring, have swept away a great deal that was obstructing our forward advance. We must make use of the situation that has developed to speed up the solution of all our problems. One might say that it was a sort of emergency stop on the way and that now we must move forward with even greater determination, and make full use of the new historical chance that has opened up before the country.

As a person who headed the Communist Party of the Soviet Union since 1985 I cannot avoid the question of the attitude to communists. My position is this: I am a resolute opponent of whipping up anti-communist hysteria or allowing the persecution of millions of communists, honest people who have done nothing to stain their reputations. For a long time I really did think that the CPSU could be reformed. But the August coup destroyed those hopes. I realized that a short time after my return from the Crimea.

It turned out that people in the leadership of the Party, primarily in the Secretariat of the Central Committee, did not have the courage to speak against the coup and in defence of the Constitution of the Union and of the General Secretary and to insist on a meeting with him. Having in essence supported the Committee for the Emergency they led the Party astray and set it off on a fatal path. Many Party committees decided to help the plotters.

In speaking of the responsibility of the leading bodies I think it highly important to distinguish the millions of rank and file members of the Party from the Party bureaucracy. I said this at once, as soon as I had an opportunity to do so, on 22 August. I am repeating myself, but I shall say once again: the coup wiped out any hope of reforming the CPSU and turning it into a modern, democratic party. That is why I resigned the post of General Secretary and proposed that the Central Committee should dissolve itself.

The Parties in the republic are being reorganized and their programmes and names are being changed. It is possible that in time two major parties will form in our country – socialist and democratic. The most important thing is that rank and file communists who had nothing to do with the coup should be able to make their choice independently and without any pressure on them.

I am one of those who have never concealed their convictions. I am a confirmed supporter of the idea of socialism. It is an idea that has been making a way for itself for many centuries. It has many supporters and they have headed the governments of a number of states. There are various branches of the socialist movement, because it is not a kind of model into which society has to be driven. No, it is an idea, precisely an idea, which embraces values developed in the course of a search for a juster society and a better world. It is an idea that draws strength from many achievements of Christianity and from other philosophical tendencies. The idea of socialization is present in many social and political movements.

I consider myself to be a democrat and I base my thinking on the assumption that the socialist idea without democracy and without a correct and reliable solution of social problems is not possible. In discussing socialism we must recognize that it was the model of socialism that we had in our country which proved a failure, and not the socialist idea itself.

The question is sometimes asked: was the October Revolution a catastrophe or was it after all a genuine revolution? I understand why such a question arises – because its historical results were not those that the people who made the revolution counted on. But they were not the results of carrying through the ideas of October, a genuine people's revolution. They were the results of the forcible imposition of the Stalinist model of society. One must not confuse the two things.

As for my own views, I have done everything through the years to put an end to Stalinism. Without that there is no point in even thinking about realizing the socialist idea. Life in every country must be the work of the people themselves. It is now our duty to extend and develop the processes of democratization in all spheres. I think it all amounts to a movement towards greater justice for the individual and the affirmation of his rights and freedoms and the rights and freedoms of the peoples. And that really is a movement in the direction of realizing the socialist idea. Such is my understanding of the problem.

In some especially fierce speeches after the August events there could be heard demands that the Supreme Soviet and the government of the Russian Federation and the Supreme Soviets and governments of other republics should expel socialism from the territory of the Soviet Union. A very dangerous Utopia. That no one will succeed in achieving that is clear. It is also clear that it is just one more variant of the Crusades, of religious wars in today's style, capable of provoking civil strife.

We have declared freedom of belief and political pluralism in our country. To set the task of driving socialism from the territory of the Union means to call for a 'witch-hunt'. The individual determines his own position and chooses the movement or party he favours or remains outside movements and parties altogether. Such is the principle of freedom of choice to which we have pledged allegiance. And it must be strictly observed in our life.

The Emergency Session
of the Supreme Soviet
of the USSR

As I prepared for the session, which opened on 26 August, I saw myself faced with two cardinal tasks.

In the first place, in spite of everything, we had to achieve a strengthening of the rule of law and of legal order. Any other approach was simply inadmissible and unacceptable. It was understandable that people felt their anger was justified. But it was not right to set out under its influence on the path of unrestrained lawlessness. That would compromise the victory over the plotters and would actually operate in favour of those who wanted to cause trouble.

Justice demands an assessment of the behaviour of those officials who could have put up some resistance to the attempted coup but failed to do so, who took up a waiting attitude or were even ready to bow to the demands of the criminal Committee for the Emergency. Since they did not find in themselves the courage to take a stand in defence of the law and did not resign as a sign of protest, let them do it now.

But after all that has happened we must not embark on a course of persecuting people and acting as people acted in former times. No – we must remain within the framework of democracy and *glasnost*, moving towards a state based on the rule of law.

In a word, I do not accept indiscriminate accusations. We

must analyse each case separately; that is the only way. There must be no leniency, but there must also be no ignoring of the law. We must not permit any settling of accounts with political opponents or persecution for thinking independently or for belonging to one political organization or another. Our society, which lived through monstrous repression under Stalin's regime, is particularly sensitive to such things.

In the second place I considered the most important thing was to revive the process connected with the Union treaty. The conspirators had succeeded in having the signing of the treaty, set for 20 August, called off. Along with the declaration issued by the so-called Committee for the Emergency on 19 August a statement by Lukyanov was published and was later, as I learnt, transmitted repeatedly by the mass media. In it he tried to prove that the treaty was no good and ought not to be signed.

But the draft treaty represented a balance of interests between all the participants of the Novo-Ogarevo agreement. I agreed with the proposals made in speeches by the leaders of the Russian Federation and by participants in the meeting of representatives from Leningrad and from the north-west of Russia: not to delay the signing.

At a meeting with leaders of nine republics on 23 August, on the second day after my return from the Crimea, the predominant opinion was that the treaty should be signed as quickly as possible, that it should not be long delayed. I want to emphasize that it was not a question of finalizing the process but only of beginning the profound transformation of our Union.

Perhaps the most tragic result of the attempted coup is that those three days stimulated, gave a real boost to the centrifugal tendencies in the country. There emerged a real threat that the state would fall apart and no longer be a union. I think about this constantly and with a tremendous feeling of anxiety and concern. Because, if that were to happen, then all our talk and all our plans for the future would be just thin air, mere chatter.

I put that question in the foreground as the most important and fundamental, particularly since I heard a lot of comments of this kind: let us, they say, carry on like this, go separate ways and then come together again.

Everybody was in favour of our having a single system of defence and common armed forces. That does not mean that in some places, say in Russia, there cannot be a national guard of some three or four thousand men that would be needed in such situations where the security of the parliament was threatened or something like that. That is another question. But in principle, we need common armed forces and a common economic market. In short, there was agreement that the necessary amendments should be made to the draft treaty and that the process of signing it should be begun.

The session greeted this announcement with applause. At the same time a different view was to be heard clearly during the debate: get rid of the Union treaty – we were already, it was said, in another country and another epoch. Of course, we could not ignore what had taken place in those August days. Amendments were necessary – amendments that would take into account the tragic experience we had gained and the lessons drawn from what had happened. I considered it essential that the leaders in the republics that were in favour of the treaty should immediately deal with that. Particularly since by then an understanding had been reached to start at once the drafting of an economic agreement between the republics.

Consequently I spoke out very clearly at the Supreme Soviet session in favour of introducing changes in the draft Union

treaty. Not to react to the situation in which we found ourselves and pretend that everything was back where it was
before 18 August – that would really be no policy at all. But
we could not throw out everything we had gained by the
Novo-Ogarevo process and what we had done before that. That
would be a mistake.

We had not yet separated or disintegrated: we had only
allowed the links between the republics to weaken and a confrontation to begin. Previous relations had been disrupted.
And what state was the country in as a result? What might a
refusal to sign the Union treaty lead to? What would happen
if the republics began to reject the Union categorically, if
hastily and in an emotional atmosphere we set about solving
the exceptionally complicated problems involving the fate of
this vast state which it had taken a thousand years to shape?
And involving the fate of tens of millions of people, their civil
rights, frontiers, and the ownership of public property and
wealth created through the labours of the whole people?

No: we had to work together, to create within the framework of a Union state a single democratic, economic, scientific,
technological and cultural space, to cool our passions but not
on any account to alter frontiers. Otherwise there would be a
growth of separatism and the situation would be difficult. We
must know where to stop.

Even during the course of the session I had meetings with
Yeltsin, Akayev (President of Kirghizstan), Nazarbayev and
Aleksandr Yakovlev. We discussed the meaning of what was
happening in Moscow and around the capital and what was
going on in all the regions. The situation was tense, there
was uneasiness throughout the country: people were worried,
concerned about what would happen to them and to the
country and what lay ahead. We exchanged opinions and
agreed to inform the members of the Supreme Soviet of our

common position. It amounted to this: that the Union state should be preserved as a Union of Sovereign States.

I assured the Deputies that I would do everything in my power to make sure that the line would not be crossed beyond which the collapse of our Union would become inevitable. The situation was such that we needed a Union of Sovereign States. That formula had to be the basis for preparing the treaty, taking account, of course, of our more recent experience. I was in favour of a renewed Union, a radically reformed Union, but I was for preserving the Union and carrying out the will of the people as expressed in the referendum on 17 March. And if that didn't come about, if there was going to be something different, then I would quit. We were bound to fail if we destroyed the Union. I assure you: it would be a disaster.

Somebody voiced the suspicion that I was allegedly instigating something, that I was making speeches aimed at splitting the country up, setting the peoples against each other so as to rule over them, and more of that sort of thing. And there were also people who saw in the stand I took a striving at all costs to preserve the empire. It was all rubbish.

When I analysed the processes that had been started in our country because of language problems and because some other problems, such as the cultural questions, had been left unresolved – that appeared at first sight to be unimportant but which touched people on the raw – I realized that, if we tried meddling with more serious issues, the country would start to break up and forces would emerge with which we could not cope. Having thought this over I came to the firm conviction that we must not split up, but that we must distribute and divide up our powers and reform the Union profoundly. Let the centre be as the republics themselves want it to be. But let us keep together. We can then make our way out of the crisis and overcome everything together and so recover. We have everything, and we can now rely on the accumulated potential of *perestroika* and move quickly on along the path of reform.

There was a time when no attention was paid to many things and whole regions were transferred from the control of one republic to another. Anyway, it was said, it was all in the same state, what did it matter? Problems arose sometimes as local issues, but in most cases they were quickly settled – since, after all, we were all together! But behind the façade of the policy that proclaimed the 'friendship of the peoples' and even the 'merging' of nations together quite a few problems accumulated.

We have now come to realize a lot of things. We take seriously the possibility that some of the republics will not want to sign the treaty, that is to say they will take the path of secession. But let it all be done within a constitutional framework. If a republic leaves the Union there will arise a whole complex of problems that it will be essential to examine – legal, humanitarian, territorial, military, economic and so on.

At the session of the Supreme Soviet I set out my views of what the new Union would look like. I took the view then and I take it now that relationships within the Union should be built on a foundation of agreements and treaties embracing questions of defence and of the economy, and especially questions of citizens' rights. There will have to be a whole system of agreements. It is possible that even territorial questions will arise. But the draft of the Union treaty says that 'frontiers are inviolable'. This theme has been present at all the meetings in the last three or four months and everybody always expressed his or her position clearly and simply: that frontiers must be inviolable. That is understandable, especially since, living in a unified Soviet Union we did not really know properly where our internal frontiers ran, because seventy per cent of them were fixed by district soviets and those in the villages and towns.

In the renewed and reformed Union the republics themselves will set up new union bodies with such powers as the Union invests in them.

My appeal was that, as a result of the debate in the Supreme Soviet, there should ring out a clear and precise attitude towards the future of our Union, that everything should be thought through carefully so that the Union can be preserved and continue to develop in the interests of the peoples of those republics that have decided to preserve it and to sign the Union treaty. My appeal was heard by the Deputies.

I appealed to the members of the Supreme Soviet representing the voters in Russia to use their authority and the opportunities that had opened before them with the aim of uniting the country into a new Union. At the same time I considered it essential to say to the Deputies from the other republics that they should not harbour any suspicions concerning the Russian people. Respect for other peoples was typical of Russians and would continue. Passing incidents should not be allowed to conceal what history, centuries of history, had taught us.

Practically all the speakers at the session voiced anxiety about the fact that the attempted coup had made it more difficult to administer the country and had undermined the already weakened interaction between the republics and regions. That really was true. That is why at the session I raised as the second very important task that we should act firmly to preserve and strengthen our ability to administer the country. We had to address quickly all the problems life had presented us with; we had to act but not to wreck. We had to promote new people to the government bodies, people whom we trusted and whom the country would follow. We needed a regrouping of political forces, the creation of Union bodies for a transitional period, and then, in the next few months, free elections to set up new structures of power.

Why did I raise so sharply the problem of the administration, of not allowing things to run out of control? Because it is a question of providing adequate food supplies, fuel and employment, and of continuing the reforms.

Here I must speak of my deep satisfaction that the tendency prevailed at the session not to permit acts of political revenge, any persecution of people for their opinions, their dismissal from their employment or depriving them of a defence. The Deputies were unanimous: the rule of law and the maintenance of legal order were essential. Then we shall stay on track. I spoke in support of an initiative by Deputies who are professional lawyers, who called upon the Supreme Soviet to distinguish clearly between what has to be established by the investigators and the courts and what comes under the heading of political assessments and personnel changes. I also supported a proposal to set up a parliamentary commission which would take part in that process.

Many Deputies at the session subjected me to harsh criticism, which was not unfounded. It was painful to listen to, but necessary. I considered it my duty to declare again and again that as President I was deeply upset by what had happened. I felt my responsibility before all the Deputies for the fact that I had not done everything possible to prevent the August coup. I did not think it possible then nor do I think it possible today, to minimize, gloss over or evade it. More than once during those days I spoke openly and in detail about my attitude to what took place and my assessment of the causes of what had happened.

But I considered it necessary to point out that the putsch

was defeated both within the country and outside it. But that would not have happened without the profound changes in the country and in its international relations. And, after all, all that was not done without my participation.

That is why I declared quite categorically in a television interview on the evening of 1 September, on the eve of the opening of the extraordinary Congress of People's Deputies:

'I am not now going to submit my resignation. It would be an immoral act, even if other aspects are not taken into consideration. I will not allow myself, as a person and as a citizen, to quit now at this most difficult stage when decisions have to be taken which will determine whether the course that we set out on in 1985 will be preserved. Therefore I will not submit my resignation. As for the Congress, let it debate the question. I shall find what to say; I have things to say to the Congress.'

The Congress of People's Deputies

The situation is developing very quickly. We don't have time even to grasp everything that is happening. It could be said that in one day we live through decades. That also applies to the development of the situation in the republics. There were, I repeat, nuances of difference in the stands they took, but the 'Committee' did not succeed in dragging them into its intrigue. But as a result of the coup centrifugal tendencies made themselves clearly felt. Some people got the idea that to resist similar turn-rounds in the centre they should break off links with the Union.

But, in reply to the threat of a chaotic collapse, another tendency at once became apparent – aimed at stopping the disintegration. We had to apply tremendous efforts and to act very resolutely.

It is now evident that, despite the considerable spread of opinions, the tendency to support the Union and a single economic market has been preserved.

At the same time it is notable that statements heard frequently at the sessions of the Supreme Soviets of the republics did not always reflect the mood of the whole population. In those anxious days we became convinced that a majority of the people were very sensitive to the threat of the Union falling apart. And, unlike the nationalists and anarchists, that majority came to regard the acquisition of independence as the basis for a new Union of genuinely sovereign and independent states. At that dangerous moment for our multinational state people of various nationalities sensed especially keenly that we needed to hang together. That had a decisive effect on the process of harmonizing the positions of the republics on the eve of the extraordinary Congress of People's Deputies of the USSR.

The Joint Declaration by the President of the USSR and the leaders of the republics – the '10(11) plus 1'* – was drawn up literally in a single day. I would even say in a single night, before the Congress began its work. We were working on it to the very last moment. Nazarbayev read out at the Congress a text in which the last corrections were in longhand. Not only the nine republics which had participated in the Novo-Ogarevo process plus the President but also Armenia and Georgia took part in that work.

We saw the point of the Declaration in the fact that we were going to the people with proposals concerning the most pressing and disturbing questions. We argued like this: the Congress ought not to be allowed to turn into a parliamentary talking shop. The country was looking for decisions. That was why we took such an unusual path – to present a Declaration. And we told the Deputies: now think about it, give some thought to the future.

Of course, this gave rise to discontent at first. But, after all, we had to extract ourselves from the situation resulting from the conspiracy and not just chatter.

The Congress now had a chance to show its sense of responsibility for the country's fate. If it had not accepted that proposal it would have demonstrated to the whole people that it was dead.

---

* Leaders of eleven republics and the President of the Soviet Union drafted the declaration. Ten republics formally supported it.

The Declaration called for the conclusion without delay of a treaty on the Union of Sovereign States.

We recorded in the Declaration the fundamental principles of the new treaty with all the attributes of a Union. It provided for a single economic space, common armed forces and military reform, and called for a confirmation of all international obligations and a declaration concerning the freedoms and rights of the individual.

The Congress took place in an atmosphere of public shock and itself reflected that atmosphere. Nevertheless it turned out to be equal to its mission. After sharp debates agreement was reached on what was most important.

There was a moment when we reached a stalemate situation. So I put the issue in a straightforward way: the Congress has exhausted its possibilities, and if that is the case we shall have evidently to seek other machinery for taking the decisions that the people are waiting for, because people can't wait any longer.

In the end the Congress took important decisions. But it was hard going. The atmosphere at the Congress changed literally day by day. I would say that in three days everything changed; a new life and a new epoch began.

During the past several weeks the people were deciding their fate, not only in parliaments and public clashes of opinions at rallies, but, unfortunately, also at the barricades. A tragedy took place, bathed in blood. What had happened was for all of us a very hard lesson. Everybody can see the dramatic nature of the situation in which the country has found itself as a result of the anti-constitutional *coup d'état* carried out at a moment when there was only a day to go before the signing of the treaty on the Union of Sovereign States. The treaty would have opened up the possibility of consolidating accord and collaboration. Now time had also been lost for the solution of vital economic problems. Social tension in the country was at its limit. But at the same time what had happened confirmed with irrefutable persuasiveness that what we have been doing since 1985 had permitted the creation of such preconditions and new realities in the country that the conspiracy was doomed from the very outset.

Replying to a question put to me at the Congress, I said: As far as it is a question of commitment to the policy of revolutionary and profound change in all spheres of life in our society, you are looking at the very same Gorbachev. But while he has remained fully committed to his main choice of 1985 Gorbachev has changed; he has understood and felt deeply his mistakes both in tactics and in his methods of acting. One of them was not to recognize that the moment had come when we should quickly have liberated society from the machinery supporting the totalitarian system. He was not able in good time and in full measure to assert his authority to unite the new democratic forces which could have taken upon themselves all responsibility for carrying through the policy of *perestroika*.

Our society is now overexcited. It wants to understand fully what happened. What were the sources of what took place? What must be done so that such a thing should never be repeated? What is the way out of the situation that has arisen, and where are the institutions and the people who will assume responsibility at this enormously difficult time? These are the questions that are now tormenting people. That was actually the reason for calling the extraordinary session of the Congress of People's Deputies and for the Declaration made by the President of the country and the top leaders of the Union republics.

I appreciate very highly the fact that, although they expressed a great variety of opinions, the majority of the

People's Deputies treated our assessment of the situation with a great sense of responsibility and in principle supported the Declaration.

But I cannot agree with those speeches in which the Declaration was depicted as being at odds with the Constitution and the laws of the country and, moreover, treated almost as if it were yet another coup. My reply was simple: attempts to present actions aimed at the defence of democracy and at ensuring that immediate steps are taken to save the country as some 'dark plot' against the people, and to describe as impostors people who have been legally elected and are backed by millions of voters and the parliaments of the republics – this is impermissible and must be rejected resolutely.

Just how absurd it all is is shown by the fact that the President and the leaders of the republics presented their Declaration to the Congress, the supreme organ of state power and a constitutional body, and not to anyone else. They appealed to the Congress and to its constitutional authority. Does that sound like the behaviour of conspirators?

It is also interesting to note that people of the extreme right and those from the extreme left came together in criticizing the Declaration. It was amazing to observe this. But in the end the Congress did the right thing and opened a door into the future, and that marked the beginning of a difficult transitional period.

It is, of course, possible to find fault with the decisions taken, and lawyers have complained about the procedure of the debate. But that is not what is most important.

We live at a time when unusual steps have to be taken and unusual decisions to be approved. It is of fundamental importance that in a situation when the coup had brought the country to the brink of an unmanageable collapse, the leaders of eleven republics considered it necessary to meet and worked out agreed positions on the fundamental problems in the life of society and obtained the support of the Congress.

It was clear to me and to the leaders of the republics that to re-establish the country's administration it was essential to have an authoritative body capable not only of taking decisions but also of ensuring that they were put into practice throughout the territory. For that reason we proposed that the Congress should create for the transitional period a State Council that would include the highest officials of the republics.

A very sharp debate developed at the Congress over a proposal to set up a Council of Representatives, a sort of legislative assembly for the period of transition. Serious arguments and objections were put forward. All of us, the authors of the Declaration, took these reactions very seriously and came to the conclusion that our idea could be put into practice, not through the Council of Representatives, but through the Supreme Soviet according to a formula that had been written into the draft of the new Union treaty. That provided for two chambers, including a Council of the Republics, and the interests of the former autonomous republics and regions were taken into account. Moreover, in the upper chamber, the Council of the Republics, which would be the higher one, each republic would have one vote.

I conveyed this agreed opinion to the Deputies, stressing that on that basis it would be possible to create a body which would collaborate effectively with the State Council. In other words, in this case we would not be going outside the framework of the Novo-Ogarevo process but at the same time would have what would be essentially a qualitatively different parliament corresponding with the needs of the transitional period.

The most important thing now was to move fast. It

was the Russian prime minister, Ivan Silayev, who rightly reminded the Congress that there were urgent problems connected with food supplies, with preparations for the winter, with law enforcement, and with the financial situation – and they all required agreed action. And there were the preconditions for keeping the situation in hand and moving forward.

If we succeed in organizing joint action in new forms and get down to work with new bodies and new people, then the West will support us. The West is now seeking to know with whom to deal. That is why, both because of the internal processes and for cooperation with the outside world (and that is essential for us) all these problems should be addressed without delay.

Again at the Congress I stressed strongly the need to clear up urgently the question of our state system. If we do not clear that up we shall not resolve other questions – economic, political, social, scientific, inter-ethnic and so forth. I am convinced of that. In the March referendum the people expressed their will and voted for the preservation and resolute renewal of the Union. In the course of the Novo-Ogarevo process we arrived at the formula – a Union of Sovereign States – but that too is now in need of reinterpretation.

Let us, I said, make this Union genuinely voluntary, so that it will suit everybody's interests. Let it offer the possibility of having federative links as regards certain questions, confederative in other cases and associative in still others. The formula – a Union of Sovereign States – allows everything to be taken into account. If we do that, if the Congress supports the proposals that are stated in the Declaration, it will fulfil its role at this historically critical moment.

To a certain extent it was a landmark, even a turning-point; in what was fundamental and most important the position of the President and the leaders of the republics won the approval of the overwhelming majority of the Deputies. The final outcome of the Congress was a package of decisions regulating the life of the state for the period of transition. They lay a foundation for stabilization and the conduct of affairs along a normal course. There is agreement between the republics and the Union that their collaboration will be built at a new level by all of us together, jointly.

That was why, in closing the Congress, I declared myself satisfied with the work we had done. Although, speaking frankly, there had been moments when I thought we would not make it through to the logical conclusion.

It is not often in political life that there are days and weeks that can literally be called historic. The country went through just such a moment. It marked the beginning of a new epoch in its thousand-year development.

I believe and am quite convinced that the international community will be dealing with a Union of Sovereign States, with a country in which free democratic states and republics and dozens of nations and national and ethnic groups cohabit voluntarily and with equal rights − a country in which the most varied cultures and practically all known religions exist side by side and interreact, creating a unique cultural and spiritual entity.

The great Eurasian democracy will become one of the bulwarks of the new world, of its security and of the *rapprochement* of two continents in building a just world order. The combined foreign policy potential of the new Union will increase thanks to the liberated and original contribution that will be made by the sovereign republics that compose it. All that is, of course, ahead of us. But we shall work persistently and consistently, keeping that objective in sight.

The Declaration of the rights and freedoms of the individual, which was approved by the Congress, and the documents defining the guidelines for the transition period and the principles underlying the new Union take as their starting point the recognition that freedom of the individual, his honour and dignity are the highest values in our society. That becomes the moral and, what I particularly want to stress, the legal foundation of our Union.

The point to which the Congress has brought the country is not in any way something unexpected or in contradiction to the general direction of *perestroika*. On the contrary, there has taken place an explosive release of all that potential for social, economic and national development that has accumulated in the course of *perestroika*. From the very beginning of *perestroika* our main idea was to build on that potential.

So basically everything that has been opened up and the developments now taking place in our country correspond with my deepest convictions and intentions.

There remained one problem of exceptional importance, the solution of which was actually predetermined by the result of the Congress. I have in mind the problem of the Baltic republics — Lithuania, Latvia and Estonia — which announced that they did not wish to sign the new Union treaty and that they wished to leave the Union.

This problem was discussed on the day following the Congress, at the first meeting of the State Council. Bearing in mind the actual historical and political situation preceding the entry of Lithuania, Latvia and Estonia into the USSR, the State Council recognized their independence and authorized a plenipotentiary state delegation to conduct negotiations and resolve the whole complex of problems connected with securing citizens' rights and also economic, political, military, frontier, humanitarian and other problems.

From the political and practical points of view it was clear that events had been leading towards withdrawal of the three republics from the Union. Recent developments speeded up the solution.

I must say, however, that I have been literally swamped by telegrams from the Baltic states. After all, 2.5 million of the 7 million population of the three republics do not belong to the indigenous population. If extremist emotions should prevail, and there is evidence of them, and if they start squeezing out and expelling the non-indigenous inhabitants, then we shall have a very dangerous situation on our hands. A discussion is now taking place there concerning the laws of citizenship. Some people are talking about dividing citizens into several different categories. That causes alarm in the country and is really dangerous.

After decisions had been taken by the State Council I had talks with Ryuitel and Gorbunov (the leaders of Estonia and Latvia) and stressed that they ought to give this question very close attention. Anyway, it seems that people in the Baltic states have recently begun better to understand the situation and their own responsibility. After all, we intend to go on living together, to live at peace with each other.

Until the beginning of 1992 we do not intend to change anything in our collaboration, in our economic, including financial, relations. Like others, Latvia, Lithuania and Estonia are interested in obtaining economic resources from other parts of the Union. And the other regions of the Union have a similar interest in relations with the Baltic states. There was good reason for officials from the Baltic states to take part in the work of Grigori Yavlinksy's commission for preparing the Economic treaty. In the future our relations will be based on that treaty and on agreements on specific questions relating in particular to the use of ports and communications, the presence of troops, the electricity grid, and so forth.

I am convinced that in the course of negotiations we shall be able to decide everything as it should be. We expect a constructive approach on the part of the leaders of the Baltic states – especially since Latvia, Lithuania and Estonia have already acquired the status of independent participants in the CSCE (the Conference on Security and Cooperation in Europe) and have become members of the United Nations. It is clear that a greater degree of responsibility now lies on other states, and primarily the European states, for the way these countries settle down in the world community, and in particular for the fate of the considerable minorities in each of the Baltic countries. Any retreat from the criteria laid down in the Paris Charter in this regard might provoke a very unpleasant reaction, not only in those countries themselves, but in Russia and the Union too.

Within the framework of the CSCE process some system will certainly be worked out for securing the rights of all citizens. But there are matters that are of primary importance and among them above all is the inviolability of frontiers. We must move towards ensuring the openness of borders, but we must not meddle with the frontiers themselves. That could lead to the gravest consequences.

We shall continue to collaborate with the Baltic states. Our attitude is extremely constructive: after all, the people living on the other side of the new frontiers are people close to us with whom we have had links for centuries. We want the rules governing exchanges, visits and contacts to be as simple as possible. It is important that everything should be done in a civilized way, with mutual respect as between good neighbours. I hope that everything in our relations with those states will go well.

The Contours of the
New Union

The Congress is over, but the work involved in the formation
of what is fundamentally a new Union of Sovereign Republics
that constituted the former USSR is only just beginning.
Again there are debates and conflicts between the various
points of view. The argument has flared up in essence between the supporters of federation, of confederation and
of association. At the outset it was difficult even to suggest
anything that would unite the sides in that argument. I
put forward again the formula – that we should create a
Union of Sovereign States, on the assumption that that would
make it possible to establish a new balance between the
centrifugal and centripetal forces. It would create a new
union state.

Such a Union, as I see it, will ensure collaboration between
all of its subjects in the interests of the peoples who compose it. Various kinds of links can exist between them. The
formula of a Union of Sovereign States creates possibilities
that open up the way to resolve all problems while taking
into account the opinions of every people in each republic.
Apart from that, it will make it possible to find the opti-
mum way to combine the sovereignty of the parts and of
the whole.

The new Union must undoubtedly be founded on the principles of independence and territorial integrity for itself and

the states that belong to it. It must include the right to join the Union and the right to leave it.

In this way the future Union treaty will define the actual outlines of the shape of a great new entity. It is not simply a matter of continuing the Novo-Ogarevo process. In the course of drafting the treaty account will be taken of the new realities that have become so clearly apparent and made themselves felt in connection with the events of 18–21 August. Among them is the understanding that was gaining ground rapidly at the beginning of September that the acquisition of independence was not an excuse for a chaotic rupture of historic links but a new foundation for creating a stable Union of really sovereign and genuinely independent states.

Russia has an especially great and responsible part to play. On 10 September Boris Yeltsin and I had a meeting at which we discussed problems connected with the urgent drafting of a new version of the Union treaty. And on 16 September the question of the future Union was the subject of a discussion between members of the State Council. Eight republics took a positive attitude then – the Russian Federation, Byelorussia, Uzbekistan, Kazakhstan, Turkmenistan, Azerbaidjan, Tadzhikistan and Kirghizstan.

The situation in the Ukraine remains complicated. I am a convinced supporter of the preservation and development of the Ukraine within its existing frontiers. I cannot imagine that it will come to the Ukraine's secession. Moreover, I see it playing an indispensable role in the formation of the new Union. I am sure that the formula of a Union of Sovereign States will make it possible to come to terms about everything.

An important factor in ensuring the integrity of the Union will be the single armed forces, effective centralized control over the nuclear potential, and a joint defence policy. That will provide a guarantee of dependable security for all the republics and the Union as a whole. At the same time it will correspond to the fundamental principles of current international politics.

The leaders of most of the republics reached agreement in principle not only on the need for unity of the strategic forces but of the armed forces in general. As for control over the nuclear weapons, no one should have any worries on that account. The centre and the President as supreme commander-in-chief remain.

There is, of course, need for a profound military reform. We are going to have a civilian minister of defence and a military man as chief of the joint or general staff. There will be some organizational changes, and in cooperation with the republics we are going to reduce the size of our forces. Taking account of where the units are stationed machinery is needed for mutual understanding and collaboration with the republics. Consultations are already under way.

A second support for the Union we are building is the Economic treaty. A draft of it was studied in the State Council on 16 September.

The Economic treaty is what we now need urgently; it will also stimulate work on the Union treaty. The Economic treaty records the republics' support for maintaining a single market, and defines the norms and machinery for the functioning of the single economic space, which will make it possible to speed up the economy's recovery from the crisis. Work on the Economic treaty has now entered its final phase, and fully authorized delegations from the republics are taking part in the work.

The situation looks like this: the republics are eager to conclude the Economic treaty, and that is understandable. Even Russia cannot manage without cooperation with other republics, and the smaller republics even less so. The way the economy is structured, with a single raw material base, a single scientific community, the same ecology, power networks and multifarious economic links – all this determines the logic of collaboration.

In the next few months already we are faced with the task of carrying out jointly major steps aimed at the stabilization of our finances, at creating conditions for entrepreneurial activity, and at privatization and phasing out state property. Apart from that, there will of course be worked out the principles for a common policy in the field of taxation, banking, social problems and so on.

Some republics raise the question of having their own currency. They argue that it would give them protection against negative economic tendencies and would protect their local, republican markets. Our economists consider that the introduction of national currencies would not present serious problems, especially since achieving convertibility of the rouble will check the rush to have separate currencies. Many foreign economic and financial institutions warn against such moves, which are liable seriously to complicate the operation of the market. In any case I presume that the rouble will play a leading role, bearing in mind the size and importance of a republic like Russia.

Now we have to start moving along parallel courses: the creation of a new Union treaty and a new economic union based on such principles as will contribute to progress towards a free market. The attitude of the people to these questions has recently changed for the better. That is of exceptional importance.

The third direction of work on the new Union is the creation of a Union government structure appropriate to the changed conditions. There has already been some progress here. The possibility is opening up of overcoming the general crisis. We have been given a greater degree of credibility than we had before the coup.

Following approval of the 10(11) plus 1 Declaration some practical steps were taken. Having dissolved the Cabinet of Ministers we decided to retain, in addition to the Ministry of Foreign Affairs, the Ministry of Internal Affairs, the Ministry of Defence and the Committee for State Security as Union bodies.

Then we reconstructed the Union Ministry of Culture in a new form. I had meetings with the leaders of ministries of education in the republics. They were all insistent in their efforts to persuade me that it was essential to coordinate the work of the republics in a single educational framework, for the whole of the Union. I received a letter from the ministers of agriculture of practically all the republics suggesting that we should set up some Union structures for agricultural matters. The men in charge of the country's railways insist on preserving a Union ministry. Similar demands have been made with regard to ecology, and scientific and technical co-operation. The Academy of Sciences has spoken resolutely in favour of retaining a common organization for basic research.

During the transition period the bodies that were created on the basis of the decisions of the Congress of People's Deputies of the USSR must function. And they are already functioning. I have in mind primarily the State Council of the Union. It will meet regularly, not less than twice a month, and it will be responsible for taking the main political and economic decisions. The carrying out of these decisions is mandatory in the territory of the participating republics and their fulfilment can be effectively monitored.

The Inter-republican Economic Committee consisting of fully authorized representatives of the former Union republics is a body that will ensure the realization of the Economic treaty. Here will be gathered together the threads for regulating the economy and carrying out the economic programmes.

We intend to set up the appropriate machinery for carrying through the reforms, and also, on a commercial or a treaty basis, a special body for relations with foreign investors. In that way it will be easier for our enterprises to make contact with foreign partners.

The State Council and the Inter-republican Economic Committee are bodies for reaching agreement on fundamental positions. Having coordinated them the republics can act independently in specific areas and projects.

It is expected that after the Union treaty has been signed we shall define what exactly the republics should run jointly. The appropriate commissions for energy, transport, communications and other matters will be created on a basis of parity.

Such are in the most general outline the contours of the new Union. The construction work involved will not be a simple matter.

We are reaching a new stage in the development of our multinational state.

Our Country and the Outside World

In the first days following the failure of the coup we were faced with the question of whether to hold the Moscow conference for monitoring the 'human dimension' of the Helsinki process, planned for September, or to postpone it? There were then still a lot of things that were unclear. We were preparing for the Congress of People's Deputies of the USSR and clearing away the log-jams created by the putsch.

But we also understood the pressing topicality of the subject of human rights which the coup had so recently brought into question in our country. After all, the people who had fought against the conspirators were in essence defending the rights of man and the freedom gained with such difficulty in the years of *perestroika*.

We consulted with the ambassadors of the states participating in the Conference on Security and Cooperation in Europe, and we obtained from them the polite but insistent opinion – the Europeans, Americans and Canadians were all in favour of going ahead with the conference. They gave us to understand that they regarded it as their duty of solidarity with victorious democracy.

The conference opened on time on 10 September in a festive and very friendly atmosphere. It was a brilliant demonstration of what profound changes had come about in the whole nature of international relations.

We had proposed holding the conference in Moscow back at the initial stage of *perestroika*. We reckoned that it would provide an additional impulse for the democratization and renewal of our society.

At that time people in the West had many doubts as to whether Moscow was worthy of having the conference: the situation there regarding human rights was far from satisfactory, they said, although *perestroika* was already under way.

With great difficulty we succeeded in overcoming these attitudes, primarily by making practical moves to introduce into the life of our society values common to all mankind and by bringing our legislation into line with generally accepted legal standards.

And after the suppression of the putsch there no longer remained any room for doubt. Our country had changed. It became an organic part of the Helsinki process. The stereotypes of the past had melted away. In any case it was not they that determined the atmosphere in Europe.

In the speech I made at the opening of the Moscow conference I emphasized certain points related to the securing of human rights throughout our vast country in the conditions that had developed following the failure of the coup. I will summarize them.

We always knew, but now we know even better, that it is not sufficient to proclaim the rights of the individual or to announce one's support for the Universal Declaration on that subject. To become a reality the rights of man have to be secured with legislation and economic measures.

The events of August convinced us yet again of the need for reliable legal and material guarantees of the freedom of information on a national and international scale.

Under no conditions should people be subjected to persecution for holding dissenting views. We stand firmly on this position.

The transformation of the Union demands a very attentive and responsible attitude towards the national minorities in the new state entities. The process of national and state consolidation, both in the case of a republic joining the new Union and especially in the case of one leaving the USSR, must not be accompanied by any violation of the rights of minorities. Our experience in recent years forces us to be particularly attentive to this problem. But it is not only our experience.

If Europe does not want to find itself faced with a stream of refugees, armed conflicts, inter-ethnic hatred, people dying and towns and villages being destroyed, it will have to monitor very strictly the observance of the rights of the national minorities by all state entities on its territory. Otherwise the whole European process will be wrecked, burying the rights of man beneath the rubble.

The fact that a representative international forum was being held in Moscow gave me an opportunity to meet many of my old friends and partners and to discuss with them questions that were worrying us and them. A great deal of the time was, of course, devoted to discussing the situation in the Union and our plans for reform. But of course I emphasized that we regard the efforts to solve internal problems to be our most important contribution to world politics.

The fundamental course of our foreign policy remains unchanged. In their Declaration the President of the country and the leaders of the republics reaffirmed their loyalty to all international obligations. There were no differences of opinion

among us in the discussion of that point. I proposed that it
should be formulated more precisely – to say specifically that
we would be loyal to our obligations in the sphere of disarmament and foreign economic relations.

The republics that had announced their intention to form
the new Union confirmed their adherence to the policy of 'new
thinking' and to all generally accepted norms and obligations,
including those written into the Helsinki Final Act and the
Charter of Paris. They will create an effective machinery capable of ensuring an agreed line on the most important issues
of international security, disarmament and development. And
we shall review accordingly the organization and work of the
Ministry of Foreign Affairs and the embassies.

Following the defeat of the conservative forces constructive
cooperation with the United States has to rise to a new level.
In conversations with James Baker I confirmed quite definitely
our obligations and commitment to the course that we were
following together with the USA. I also pointed out that we
saw new possibilities for joint action. Even when we had our
previous institutions we were able to conclude far-reaching
treaties and agreements, but now the opportunities would be
even greater. In particular we would collaborate with the
United States, as we agreed with President Bush at Novo-
Ogarevo, in trying to settle the situation in the Middle East
by moving towards a peace conference. Here we have made a
good start.

The real prospect of turning the country into a Union of
Sovereign States radically changes the situation in Europe, too.
It must not be forgotten that, even in its previous form, the
Soviet Union acted in recent years as a powerful factor promot-
ing European security, mutual understanding and collaboration. It had not only been the originator of the idea of a
common European home but had also made a tremendous

At the 28th Party Congress, July 1990, I talk to Anatoli Sobchak,
Chairman of Leningrad City Soviet, who later left the Party and
became one of the leaders of the democratic reform movement

Prime Minister and Mrs Major welcome us at
10 Downing Street after the G7 Summit

LEFT: The meeting of the Group of 7, in mid-July 1991. The Seven plus One was a first. I met with the leaders of the seven leading industrialized countries to help integrate the Soviet Union into the world economy

BELOW: At the Group of 7 Summit – *(front row, left to right)* President George Bush, myself, Prime Minister John Major, President François Mitterrand and Chancellor Helmut Kohl; *(back row, left to right)* EC Commission President Jacques Delors and Prime Ministers Giulio Andreotti, Brian Mulroney, Toshiki Kaifu, and Ruud Lubbers

In the Kremlin, prior to our Summit talks – the visit concluded with the signing of the START Treaty

FACING PAGE: The Moscow Summit, 31 July 1991. I show the Kremlin to President Bush less than three weeks before the coup

During the visit we spend a day of informal discussions with President Bush at Novo-Ogarevo near Moscow, the same place where I hammered out the Union Treaty with the leaders of the Republics

At the Kremlin reception during the Moscow Summit – President Bush jokes with Boris Yeltsin and myself

LEFT: My press confer-
ence on 2 August with
President Bush which
concludes his visit

RIGHT: September 1991 –
I speak at the Congress of
People's Deputies. A
turning point

1.37 a.m., 20 August, in the Crimea – this photograph is
made from the videotape on which I recorded my statement

practical contribution to the positive changes taking place on the territory of Europe.

The new democratic Union of Sovereign States will take over everything positive that the Soviet Union did on the international arena and work even more actively, in all the areas foreseen by the Charter of Paris for a new Europe. For this purpose it is essential to work out together the right approach, so as not to play into the hands of the forces of separatism and national extremism, and not to upset the formation of the new Europe that has now begun and which is replacing the Europe of military alliances, confrontation and barriers that obstruct the free exchange of goods, knowledge and the achievements of science, technology and culture.

For their part the Europeans and the whole world community, who have learnt the lesson of the Yugoslav tragedy, do not conceal the fact that they are interested in preserving a single, integral state on a sixth of the globe as one of the principal guarantees of world order. Not only our state but the whole of the international community gains from this. It is true that voices are heard of those who want to have a united Union as a counterweight to a united Germany. But we see it differently: those two states can both make their own tremendous contribution to the cause of extending and deepening collaboration in Europe and the world and will be able to direct their close collaboration into a constructive channel so as to avoid shocks and chaos.

The preservation of common state structures of government and close collaboration with the West and the East are absolutely essential for transforming our country from a militarized camp into a peaceful and prosperous state. Because militarism not only drains the economy and not only prepares an ecological catastrophe, it also threatens democracy politically, physically and spiritually. That is why demilitarization is one of the most important ways of affirming human rights and freedom. We shall fight for it in our own country and elsewhere with even greater conviction and persistence.

In this connection, both in private conversations and publicly I have pointed out very clearly that we are still in favour of the speediest ratification of the Treaty on the reduction of armed forces and conventional weapons in Europe and the START Treaty on the reduction of stategic weapons.

It is impossible to be included organically into world civilization without a sound economic basis. Now that the obstacles have been removed on the path to changing the nature of our economy we can set about solving this task of gigantic difficulty. The new thinking has helped us to understand that the firm foundation for democracy lies not only in human rights and freedoms embedded in the law but also in economic freedom and a civilized modern market. It is precisely in that atmosphere that there emerges a new breed of people thinking and acting independently and ready to assume responsibility for what is happening. It is they who form the active part of civil society, the core around which new relations are formed.

But all of this, as worldwide experience shows, demands time, a great deal of time. But we have literally to break through to a new kind of society. That is why we are in need of assistance and support and solidarity. It will be more than repaid since it concerns a country on which the progress and fate of the whole world depends.

I can only add that what has been done in the days following the defeat of the coup gives us an enormous opportunity. I hope that now the West will pay greater attention to what I have said insistently and frequently in calling for practical and productive collaboration with our country.

We would be inexcusably deaf to the challenge of the hour

and to the new realities if, having been able to unite and mobilize huge resources for resolving the conflict in the Persian Gulf, we were unable to find an answer to our crisis which is of worldwide significance and which bears in itself a colossal opportunity.

A great deal depends on how the Union and the republics belonging to it behave in the transitional period. As for our external debts, all our obligations to the international community have been confirmed. We are settling up with all our partners as we always did. We have the potential to do this. The only thing that has to be remembered is that, at the present stage of rapid transition to the free market and of stabilizing measures, we need understanding on the part of the West, especially of Europe, and their readiness to meet us half-way as much as possible.

At the same time we have told our partners (and let it be heard in our country too!) that the main burden of responsibility and the main pressure of the work ahead lies on us ourselves and not on anybody else.

The main problems in the economy now are: financial stabilization and the reduction of the state budget. At the same time serious measures have to be taken to absorb the mass of excess money in circulation. On the basis of the Declaration of the country's President and the leaders of the republics the machinery has already been set up for carrying out joint, coordinated actions in the period of transition – for stabilizing economic and political life and speeding up radical democratic reforms. We aim at making the rouble convertible. We are working out practical measures to guarantee food supplies. The Inter-republican economic committee will include a major section for cooperation with the rest of the world in the field of investments.

We are interested in creating normal conditions for Western

investors. A great deal has been done here, legislation has been passed and there are many offers of cooperation.

We would like all matters of collaboration with the outside world to be based on practical machinery for joint management that will ensure the constant presence of the partner and mutual control. Then the resources allotted will not go down the drain.

Within the framework of the Union we also propose to realize the closest coordination of foreign trade policy so as to have a common approach to relations with foreign enterprises and corporations.

The changes and new elements now being introduced into our foreign trade policy are concerned with extending the republics' access to foreign markets while maintaining a common policy for foreign trade.

In a word we shall improve conditions for a speedier and a more determined implementation of the understandings reached in the framework of the Group of 7 for helping the whole Union to revive the national economy in fundamentally new conditions.

We have got to get through the coming winter. As far as fuel and energy are concerned we shall manage with our own efforts. But with food supplies we need support, literally physical support. We shall naturally pay for all that we shall get; it will be collaboration on the basis of mutual benefit.

The crushing of the attempted coup and the results of the Congress ought to remove all doubts on the part of foreign states concerning the nature of the further development of our country. The argument about when and whether we should be helped is over. It ought to be clear to everybody who bears responsibility for international policy how they should now act. So far they have done very well. They succeeded in opening up a new period in the life of our states and peoples. Now we all need to make another big effort to put oxygen into the reformation of a great country, the results of which will have decisive significance for the entire global process. Our country is now in great need of an initial push to overcome the special difficulties involved in food distribution, the functioning of light industry, the transfer to a convertible rouble and other problems connected with the transition to a market economy.

We are counting here on support, so to speak, through rapid reaction to our needs. The rest – once we have the Economic treaty which will put the country on the road to an open market – will be decided on the basis of normal collaboration with Western countries in carrying out major projects and programmes, and on the basis of the organic inclusion of the Soviet economy into the world economy.

We intend to set up a special centre which will deal with the coordination of our efforts and our cooperation with the West in training managers for work in the free market. We have received many proposals in this field but it is all very uncoordinated. We would like, along with the Americans and other partners, to establish special universities for these purposes.

Foreign policy is not an end in itself. Today, as previously, it is called upon to secure the vitally important interests of our country and our state. But our understanding of those interests and of the ways of realizing them has changed radically. Today we do not think of ourselves as being apart from the rest of the world and certainly not in any state of antagonism towards it. And the world itself looks upon us quite differently.

An historic opportunity has appeared of which we must take advantage: we must render irreversible the integration of this vast country into the community of civilized states. I do not know what the achievement of this task will cost, but I am sure that the 'price' is not to be compared with what we all paid for confrontation. The benefits will be huge and universal.

I See No Other Way But Democracy

It is amazing, but every day since those three days in August seems at times like a week. I am finishing putting in order what I have said and thought since returning to Moscow from the south, and it is just a month since the beginning of the coup. Just a month, but how much has happened, how much has changed since then.

The attempted coup was crushed. The democrats are celebrating the victory, but life demands action. It demands carefully thought through and unorthodox actions. People are discontented with the fact that their daily life is so hard and that there are no changes for the better yet. Here lies the main danger. It was precisely that which the organizers of the coup wanted to exploit. That is why there is no time to lose. We must act, push forward with the process of reform and give people economic freedom, then they will themselves realize their potential. We have a great deal to learn. We have to learn to handle the politics, the economics and the life of the state. And in that respect the democrats are still weak.

All of us have a lot to learn, so as to govern within the framework of democracy, of political and in particular economic pluralism.

Otherwise people's patience will simply be exhausted. Then there would be an uncontrolled outburst of discontent and chaos – and then just expect the worst. No less dangerous for the realization of our plans would be a reaction resulting from the people's fatigue, the spread of frustration, indifference and apathy. This might simply stop our movement towards a market economy.

I would divide into three groups the whole bundle of acute problems with which we are now confronted. In the first place there are the current problems – of providing the population with food, of organizing the efficient functioning of the fuel and energy branch of the economy, and of meeting our needs in medicines. The second group of problems concerns the creation of the conditions for the development of private enterprise and a decisive speeding up of the economic reforms. Only by proceeding in parallel in solving both groups of problems shall we be able to survive the winter and spring, obtain the desired effect from carrying out the reforms, and begin extracting ourselves from the crisis.

The most important thing now is how to survive to the spring, how to get through the winter. And all the rest, apart from these two groups of problems, is a matter of advancing more quickly to the free market and stimulating entrepreneurial activity.

But for the reforms to succeed people have to believe in them. Without people the reforms will not move off the ground, without their active participation everything will remain a dead letter. Or, on the other hand, there could be a backlash if living conditions become even worse. That would be a heavy blow struck at democracy.

I recall how, following my meeting in the Kremlin with the ambassador of the United States, I was returning to my office and was surrounded by people. We started to talk. Interestingly enough, no one was complaining about the difficulties. They said there were, of course, plenty of them, but that the people were ready to rally round, to withstand the test and support the policy of reform to the end.

We have tremendous possibilities. That is not just a standard phrase, a cliché. I am hearing it said repeatedly by foreigners whom I talk to. They say: you have everything – an educated people and huge material resources – and you can become a rich country. Yes, we must become a rich country. I repeat: we have everything we need for that. We must change. Then we shall live differently.

More than anything else I think now about how our children and my grandchildren and those who are between fifteen and twenty today are going to live. It is in that that I see the sense of my efforts, because after all it was for them that it all started. We were not frightened off by the difficulties. We knew that we were facing a lot of complicated and difficult problems. We set ourselves the objective that, today already, people should join in the democratic process and feel themselves to be real people. That has already happened. And that is an achievement of *perestroika*.

But what has to change is also our way of life and living standards. I very much wish that the people who have given so much to this land should feel that their time has come at last – a happy time.

Now, when the future of our great country is being decided, I think least of all about myself. That is why it was both a difficult moment and at the same time it was easy for me to make a decision when the plotters presented their ultimatum. I made my choice long ago. Plotters can act without bothering about the means. But I cannot try to achieve my ends by other ways . . . The choice of democracy makes it impossible for me to use any other methods. Otherwise there would inevitably be a repetition of the past, of everything we have condemned. However complicated the problems may be they must be resolved democratically. I see no other way but democracy.

Appendix A

*Transcript of the videotaped statement recorded by
Mikhail Gorbachev at the dacha in Foros on the night
of 19–20 August 1991*

I want everything I am about to say into the video camera to
be made known to the People's Deputies of the USSR, the
Supreme Soviet of the USSR and the Soviet and world public.
After listening to the press conference given by Yanayev and
other members of the so-called Committee for the Emergency
I realized that public opinion in our country and world public
opinion has been misled.

What is happening is essentially a deception with grave
consequences. Alleging that the President is in bad health and
unable to carry out his duties, the Vice-President has taken
over the duties of the President of the USSR. And on that
basis decrees are being issued and decisions taken, including
the decision to introduce a state of emergency in the country
with all the ensuing consequences.

I declare that everything said concerning the state of my
health is false. Thus on the basis of a lie an anti-
constitutional *coup d'état* has been carried out. The legitimate
president of the country has been barred from carrying out
his duties. Moreover, the house in the Crimea where I am
on holiday and from where I was due to fly today for the
signature of the Treaty on the twentieth – actually, it is
already the twentieth, and I was to take a flight on the

evening of the nineteenth – but the house is surrounded by troops and I am under arrest. I am deprived of the government communications system, and the aircraft that was here with me and the helicopters have also been sent away. I have no idea where they are. All my telephones have been cut off and I have no contact with the world outside. I am under arrest and nobody is allowed to leave the territory of the dacha. I am surrounded by troops from both the sea and the land.

I don't know whether I shall succeed in getting this out, but I shall try to do everything to see that this tape reaches freedom, as they say. You must draw the conclusion that the people, the country and world public opinion have been misled. A crude deception is being carried out before our eyes and, I would say, with unconcealed cynicism and even pleasure. And it has already led to the state of emergency to which I objected when they sent delegates to me, whom I got to know about when they had already appeared at the dacha without warning, although I had been talking with Yanayev in the middle of the day on Sunday. He checked with me the time of my flight on the nineteenth, so that he could meet me.

Most dangerous is the fact that what the Committee for the Emergency is doing now may lead to an escalation of civil conflict and confrontation, and perhaps to civil war. We all already felt that back in December, January, February and in March, and we tried then to turn everything in another direction – of agreement. We even began to see the first fruits of that agreement. Yes, there was not enough of it. Yes, it might have been different. Yes, people in power have to act and solve problems, but we must still follow the path of agreement and not the path of imposing on society a civil conflict that may set the country back and result in serious consequences for the country, the people and the whole world.

That is what I wanted to say and I ask you to evaluate it properly.

По поводу появившихся в средствах массовой информации сообщений о невозможности выполнения по состоянию здоровья М.С. Горбачевым обязанностей Президента СССР считаю своим профессиональным и гражданским долгом заявить следующее.

Являюсь лечащим врачом М.С. Горбачева с апреля 1985 года.

В последнее время существенных изменений в состоянии здоровья Михаила Сергеевича не наблюдаю. Противопоказаний по состоянию здоровья для выполнения М.С. Горбачевым возложенных на него обязанностей не вижу.

Представленным всегда готов обсудить с любой компетентной комиссией как отечественных, так и зарубежных специалистов.

19.08.91 г.   Доктор мед. наук   Борисов

(И. А. Борисов)

Appendix B

The statement of Mikhail Gorbachev's personal physician

With reference to reports that have appeared in the mass media that M. S. Gorbachev is unable to carry out his duties as President of the USSR on account of his state of health I consider it my professional duty and my duty as a citizen to state the following:

I have been M. S. Gorbachev's personal physician since April 1985.
I have observed no substantial changes in the state of Mikhail Sergeyevich's health recently. I see no reason as far as his health is concerned why M. S. Gorbachev should not carry out the duties he is invested with.

I am prepared to discuss this opinion with any competent commission of Soviet or foreign specialists.

19.8.91

Doctor of Medicine
I. A. Borisov

Appendix C

The Crimea Article*

There are two questions now worrying the country. They are at the centre of political commentaries, of scholarly discussions and of passionate debate within the Party and outside it. They are constantly present in the political struggle. The painful search for an answer to them reflects the troubled transitional time the country is going through.

First Did society need *perestroika* or was it a fatal mistake? What are its true aims? What is meant by the renewal of the state? Was it necessary to start such a risky process of transformation?

Second How are the aims of *perestroika* to be achieved, now that it has been started? What policy is to be pursued in a situation of economic crisis, dangerous signs of disintegration and chaos and of fear for the next day?

People are becoming ever more afraid lest things should go the same way as they went after the October Revolution. Lest there should again be a divergence between the great aims and the actual historical results. Could *perestroika* lead to the same kind of situation as previous generations lived through? In a situation where the standard of living is continually falling people are ever more worried: are we going the right way, using the right means, applying the right methods? In those days, in the 1920s, they also went to the limits and an historic

* Written a few days before the coup.

choice had to be made for the further advance of our great country. There was a feeling that the country would have to go through a difficult stage, but the majority of the active population had already come to the conclusion that it would have to be gone through for the sake of the 'bright future'.

But in those days they had no experience and had no results to go by. After the October Revolution and beneath its banners people kept marching towards the proclaimed objectives and never reached them. It is that which distinguishes radically the present situation. As a result of *glasnost* and the revelation of the truth a fear of major changes has entered the social memory. It nourishes in the popular mind the desire to halt, even to slip backwards so as – in that pause – to think things over yet again and maybe to start afresh. The people who do not recognize the necessity for transformation and have long been opposing it seek to exploit this. Those are the orthodox and dogmatic people, people of the past, with a stereotyped way of thinking and a limited view of things.

But among those who call upon people to halt and think again have appeared also 'leftists' of the neo-Stalinist persuasion. They appeal to people to call a halt so as to restore order by means of a dictatorship which would abolish or at best suspend all rights and freedoms that have been won in the course of *perestroika*. And once, they say, order has been restored then we shall advance to a market economy, democracy and all sorts of liberties. This point of view is gaining in popularity because the people are tired and worn out by the lack of order in life, the shortages, the uncertainty, and long just to be able to take a breather and would not object if someone turned up to put things in order from above.

Quite a lot of people might be ready to respond to that kind of appeal.

That is the soil that populism grows in. It is eagerly fertilized by would-be dictators and the apologists for Stalinism. Some of the media working on their behalf encourage this narrow-minded nostalgia for the period of stagnation when there was allegedly everything needed for daily life, not much and not the best but it was there; and as for freedom and democracy, who wants it when we've got poverty and unemployment looming? Praise for Pinochet and Franco is being offered up in earnest and publicly: just a few short years of real dictatorship, they say, and then there will be the market and democracy and prosperity and full stomachs.

The disease of populism has infected even many of the new democrats, including those who are sincere in their convictions. They too accuse the President of inconsistency, of indecision, of being too soft, and insist that 'measures must be taken'. But when the President proposes some really decisive measures for stabilizing the economy and improving our finances, the populists on the political platforms and in the corridors of power, in the towns and the republics, shy away in fright at the possibility of discontent in the population and warn of the danger of social unrest. But many of them are involved in politics and know the real possibilities and the actual state of affairs; they ought to understand that if we do not now take a number of drastic and unpopular measures aimed at achieving stabilization then from 1 January we shall have to raise prices again by two or three times. And inflation will enter a new and even more dangerous round that will condemn the country's economy to even greater disorganization.

My firm opinion is that problems can be resolved only by constitutional means. This is a source of weakness, but it is also a source of strength. The strength lies in the fact that society and the individual, having gained their freedom, have acquired the possibility of putting their democratic rights into practice, and they value that. But the weakness lies in the fact that when people abuse these rights it is very difficult to have recourse to the use of force, even if it were legitimate and justified. This is the specific nature of the process of *perestroika* as a whole. It is not a question of the President's powers but of the moral and political principle. After all, in our country everything was always decided ultimately by the use of force. Political life was conducted on this basis: if you are my opponent and I am in power you must at the very least be sent to prison. But now we have recognized the legitimacy of pluralism in the economy, in politics and in the whole of public life. But all that has yet to become a reality and it is going through a very painful birth. That is why there is need for a tremendous reserve of faith and of conviction so as not to go off the rails. That is most difficult, but essential today.

Manoeuvring of a political and an economic character is inevitable. But that does not change either the objective or the determination to achieve it by constitutional means. And no kind of pressure, either from the right or from the left, will make us depart from this.

All these years we have been forcing our way through jungles that were created long ago and that are now overrun by young plants. We have been making enormous efforts to keep on a peaceful course the new revolution in a country accustomed to the use of force and arbitrary rule. Now at last we have found an all-embracing concept of how we are to move forward. In essence it consists of a triad of interrelated basic directions which alone are capable of leading us to the objectives of *perestroika*. They are:

- the reform of the State;
- the reform of the economy;

– the country's entry into the world market and through
it and the policy of the new thinking, into the mainstream of world civilization.

With these preliminary comments I come to the subject
outlined at the beginning.

So why was *perestroika* necessary? Was it possible to have
managed without it or could it be postponed now? The majority of people now seem to believe that there can be no turning
back. But that majority also does not accept the method for
replacing the highly centralized command system – a method
which seems to be available and has been tested out in the
West: the introduction of a capitalist system throughout the
economy. But how are we to move forward, what concrete
forms and methods should be adopted that are appropriate to
the idea of *perestroika* and the directions set out by the triad?

ONE

The country is on the eve of acquiring a new structure both
as a state and as a society. Political reform has brought us to
the point where the state has not only taken on a different
form but it will also change its name. Society is rapidly freeing
itself from ideology. The monopoly of power by one party is
being replaced by pluralism. *Glasnost* and freedom of speech
have already become an indispensable feature of public life.

The economic reform has rendered irreversible the transition
to a market economy on the basis of a variety of forms of
property. Both of these reforms have opened the door for the
country to enter the world economic system according to the
'common rules of the game'.

The new thinking has contributed to such changes in the

world situation that it has become possible, at least in the principal aspects of security, to pursue a single and in the fullest sense a *global* policy. One rarely hears anyone speak of the threat of a world war.

These are the most important and most evident changes on an historical scale after six years of *perestroika*.

Is it good or is it bad?

Out of the great variety of assessments, the majority of them critical and some simply abusive, and from the huge mass of thoughts and feelings that *perestroika* had evoked in our country and throughout the world it is possible to distinguish the main question to which everybody wants an answer: is *perestroika* a revolutionary breakthrough to the natural conditions of development for a great country, or is it a catastrophe for that country and an end of its history as such?

None of the assessments should be examined apart from the time when they were actually made. They appeared in the course of the actual process of reform with *perestroika* and were a reaction to certain changes of course and to specific moves made by the authorities.

The starting point in the concept of *perestroika* was the profound conviction that we couldn't go on living as we were. I have frequently spoken about this, and I do not intend to repeat myself here. I have never, not once, regretted the fact that I was the initiator of a sharp turn in the life of our country. What came to light through *glasnost* about our past confirmed inexorably and brutally that a system created according to the rules of tyranny and totalitarianism could no longer be tolerated, not simply from the moral point of view but also from the point of view of the country's basic economic and social interests. It had already led the country into a dead end and brought it to the brink of an abyss. And it was kept in place by force, lies, fear, social apathy, and also with the assistance of artificial injections, which squandered resources and weakened potential for the future. Had we preserved the old regime for a few more years there would have been every reason to speak of the end of history for our great state.

Already in the late 1970s and early 1980s we began to feel that the economy was failing and beginning to slip back. The individual's interest in working productively had been undermined. The economy was holding back scientific and technical progress. The country found itself in a state of progressive depression.

The Stalinist totalitarian bureaucratic system had made it possible, by concentrating the strength and resources of the vast country, to achieve important results at a certain stage. But step by step the extraordinary efforts were undermining society's health. After Stalin there remained as the basis of power and of administration the very same highly centralized command system he had created, which was based on the absolute dominance of state property. That was essentially post-Stalinism.

The previous theoretical and practical model of socialism which had been imposed on the country for many decades turned out to be bankrupt. The grave crisis into which we had slid was a crisis not of any distinct parts of the social organism but of the very model of barrack-room communism.

Perestroika was thus vitally necessary; no other means existed for extricating ourselves from the vicious circle into which the country had fallen.

When we were starting our reforms we were very well aware that it was impossible to get by with a little tinkering here and there; what was needed, using Lenin's words, was one more change in our understanding of what socialism should be. But every step we took was extremely difficult because of the fact that both in the Party and in the public at large certain ideological stereotypes had taken root in the course of many decades. Society's illness turned out to be a great deal more serious than could have been supposed at the outset.

Recently I was asked: if it were possible to return to the spring of 1985, what would I want to do differently? I replied that without any hesitation I would take the same path. I was already convinced then that the reforms were vitally necessary. And the more we learnt about the true situation the country was in the more convinced we became that the reforms should have been started ten years or even twenty years previously, if not sooner. I would have preserved the basic links in the idea of *perestroika* and the basic principles and aims of the policy. Their concrete expression changed in the course of the actual political process, in the struggle, including the struggle within ourselves, with the past within us, which still has such a strong grip on all of us, some more and some less.

In the most general terms the aims of *perestroika* are: economic freedom, political freedom, escape from isolation, and the inclusion of the country in the mainstream of civilization. And the fundamental principle, if you look at it on a philosophical level, is the unacceptability of any ready-made models which might once again, however good the intentions, be imposed on society, to bring people happiness 'from above'. The aim is to emancipate the vital forces of the people themselves, to offer them the possibility in free movement to create their own well-being – each one individually and all together – and to pave the path to their future not on the basis of dogmas but guided by simple and universal human values, developed through centuries of worldwide progress.

We did not realize immediately, of course, how far we had to go and what profound changes were needed. This gave rise to mistakes: in some cases we didn't ensure that the decisions taken were synchronized, in others we were late or we moved too fast without thinking the situation through and abolished the old forms and structures without having created new machinery. Sometimes we paid too much attention to people who appeared to be appealing for reasonable restraint and caution but who were actually holding things back and putting a brake on the movement.

All that is true. But we had to get involved practically in the new work, to acquire experience, look deep into the public mind as it was found to be after seventy years of an extraordinary regime and isolation from the rest of the world, and to learn to take account of all its specific qualities. It was only then that we came to the final conclusion that *perestroika* was not to be measured by the usual criteria or directed according to the principles of a previously dominant ideology. In the end we saw also that *perestroika* would not succeed within the framework of the old system, however much we tried to renew it and improve it. What was needed was a change of the whole economic and political system, the reform of the whole multinational state; that is, in all aspects a real revolution which had been prepared by all our own past and by worldwide progress.

TWO

The first shots fired at *perestroika* came from dogmatists of a new kind who declared that there was no plan, no clear concept, and that we had set out on a path without knowing where it led. Neither now nor later will I name names, because many people later changed their views, or at least their publicly declared positions, more than once.

I always reckoned that criticism of that kind was either just demagogy or failure to think things through, a primitive way of thinking put into their heads by an essentially Stalinist intellectual education.

The person who demands at the outset that everything should be set down point by point, showing what is to be done and how, and who wants to foretell in advance all the consequences of every concrete reform embarked on, such a person is essentially an opponent of the reform of society, an opponent of *perestroika*. Because no one apart from charlatans, no academy can provide such a programme. It is up to society to give the answer. As it approaches the stage of profound reforms it 'composes its own tune', using the experience of others, but always – in its own real context – and taking into account tradition, the level of development reached, not just economic, social and scientific and technical, but also cultural, in the sense of general culture and political culture.

A second front of criticism was opened up by those people who were frightened of novelty and who declared that in general nothing substantial should have been undertaken: we had lived and would have gone on living, perhaps, without coming to any harm. The third line of criticism was that we had been right to start the process and had started it on the whole correctly, but that we later turned off the path of Marxism-Leninism. There was more to come. We soon heard shouts coming from this camp about the betrayal of socialism and that *perestroika* had been thought up specially to put an end to socialist society and to Leninism at the same time.

Some people have recently descended to the lowest level of brazenness. Just as once Lenin was accused of being a German spy who had carried through the revolution on the instructions of the German intelligence service (these ravings are now being revived), so now our yellow press seeks out among the initiators of *perestroika* agents of imperialism carrying out the plans of Western special services.

And along with that – again as happened in 1917 – a 'version' is being put around to the effect that *perestroika* is a Jewish-Masonic conspiracy. But all that comes under the heading of political schizophrenia.

As to those people in the Party and outside it who consider that *perestroika* means a betrayal of the cause of socialism, this indicates only that there is a legacy of post-Stalinism that is far from having been eliminated, that neo-Stalinism is a present-day reality, that there is a load of problems left over from the past, and that a revolution in people's minds is a very difficult process and a very slow one.

We operate in a concrete historical situation and in a real socio-political environment and we have to take account of the realities and speak the language of truth, not in hackneyed phrases from the past. No theoretical thought is worth the name if it is not based on a political analysis of the real situation. And that presupposes above all a tremendous intellectual effort, a reinterpretation of the whole of our past and of all our current activity. Our prognoses must be based on reality and not on models or designs worked out abstractly even in the very best of institutes. And if we don't stop idolizing the founding fathers – I have already spoken of this once – and if we are to continue seeking the truth in confrontation with democratic thought abroad, we deprive ourselves of the possibility of defending the idea of socialism in a modern way.

Our theoretical thinking has fallen badly behind in its understanding of developments both in our country and, especially, in the world. Abstract plans from the past and deeply implanted prejudices dominate people's minds and interfere with the process of grasping the sense of the changes taking place. But, trying to protect the dogmas of Marxism-Leninism, not making cardinal corrections in its theories by reference to the achievements of the rapidly developing science, and failing to enrich theory with the whole experience of the twentieth century, we condemn ourselves to serious mistakes in politics. And we may once again lead the country into such a jungle that we shall not only amaze but again drive the whole world away from us.

It was precisely with this in mind that the draft of a new Party Programme was prepared which has now been published and around which we must unite all the healthy forces in society who want *perestroika* to succeed.

From the very beginning *perestroika* was supported by a significant section of the intelligentsia. But in the situation where there were freedom and *glasnost*, the intelligentsia, as had already happened at times of radical change in our history, started to break up into hostile groups, many of which were soon to be found in the opposition because the country's leaders did not act as demanded by one or other of the sections of the intelligentsia.

The ultra-radicals among them, having forgotten where it all started and who to thank for bringing it about, and the sad experiences of the past, demanded that everything should be destroyed 'down to the foundations, and then . . .' Having condemned and cursed the Bolsheviks they, in effect, adopted their methodology of action.

Divisions and intolerance in intellectual circles, which are spread out over society through numerous old and new means of information, reflect, often in a distorted form coloured by hysterics and panic, the reality of society which is now going through, I would say, not just a time of troubles, but a time of turmoil.

People are looking in every direction for a way out of the situation. Some propose the complete restoration of the regime that existed under the tsar, including the monarchy. Others call for the revival of spirituality but only in one way: by identifying it with religion and handing over to the Church a monopoly of the promotion of public and personal morality. Others want to impose the capitalist system in, as they say, its 'pure form' without knowing or considering it necessary to know that an abrupt transformation of the greater part of property into private property would create a situation of primary accumulation of capital and of early capitalist development in which everyone was for himself, where people were at each other's throat, and where everyone whom success evaded should save himself as best he could.

People make ironical comments about the socialist choice but they do not see that the rejection of socialism in the public mind took place because socialism was associated with Stalinism. They do not want even for a moment to ponder the fact that the right of the idea of socialism to exist derives from the objective logic of human history. This is recognized even by anti-communist authorities – leading scholars and well known philosophers. I am convinced that the discrediting of socialism in the eyes of the masses is a passing phase. People's striving for social justice, freedom and democracy is indestructible. It is, it might be said, a global process, in the same stream as the general development of civilization. The next generation will surely return to this great idea.

Some seek salvation in repentance which is identified with a rejection of everything that happened after the October Revolution. This is a peaceful, almost religious, attitude. But there are also violent iconoclasts who do not hesitate to use the most barbarous means to destroy the memories and symbols of faith of whole generations of Soviet people who lived and fought and made sacrifices for the sake of a great idea and are not guilty of the fact that their devotion to the ideals of revolution and socialism was exploited against them with everything turning out badly.

Among the public and in particular among a section of communist officials the opinion is fairly widespread that it was on the whole correct to put an end to the Stalinist legacy and its continuation in the farce of the Brezhnev period. But now, if only there had not been mistakes in the process, if the old, tested levers of power had not been changed, and the people in whose hands they were had not been touched . . . In those circles it is the nineteenth Party Conference, in 1988, that is regarded as the most serious political mistake. That, they allege, marked the beginning of the collapse of the Party and the state. So '*perestoika* was not achieved', not having reached the objective originally set, and so 'we must turn back'.

Yes, there are many Party officials who cannot rid themselves of nostalgia. A very intelligent Spaniard I was talking to once said that if a party or some part of it values more than anything 'tokens of loyalty to their past' then they lose the basis of legitimacy in a democratic country. I will remind you once again of what I said three years ago: 'All of us, the whole Party must learn to work in a situation of increasing democracy'. To judge by everything that has happened that warning was not taken seriously. The Party has lagged behind the democratic process in society. And on those grounds it has developed an inferiority complex which has driven many into the ranks of the conservative oppositions.

Democracy is gaining ground, although the forms it takes have not solidified. Our society is living differently. Many new forces have appeared in the political arena, seeking ways, making mistakes, but wishing to do good for the country. But there are also militant and destructive forces which speak out and gain publicity and are openly reactionary and anti-communist.

All this has completely changed the political climate in the country which must be ruled by the law and only by the law, which should exclude discrimination and privilege. People must be won over in equal competition to support ideas that benefit the whole nation and our common interests. Demonstrate that you are right and consolidate society only within the framework of the law and by peaceful democratic means. And only in that way, relying on the enlightened majority, can we repudiate and curb the attempts of all sorts of nationalistic, chauvinistic, adventurist and similar elements. Otherwise there will be disaster.

Yes, those forces want to knock the country's leaders off balance. And when they fail to get what they want through constitutional channels they operate through the crowd, resorting to mob rule, incitement and the exploitation of difficulties. This phenomenon can now be observed also in Party circles. It is the way to switch the Party to the side opposite to *perestroika*. But for communists, if they want to remain an influential political force of the socialist persuasion, there is no alternative but to seek answers along the paths of continuing and extending the reforms whose aim is to bring about a radical renewal of society and to modernize it. There is no other way out of the crisis for us but to unite all the patriotic forces and all the democratic movements for the solution of nationwide tasks. For that purpose we must collaborate and, where necessary, reach a compromise with other political forces.

The introduction of a state of emergency, in which even some supporters of *perestroika*, not to mention those who preach the ideology of dictatorship, see a way out of the crisis, would be a fatal move and the way to civil war. Frankly speaking, behind the appeals for a state of emergency it is not difficult sometimes to detect a search for a return to the political system that existed in the pre-*perestroika* period.

Among the collection of critics and oppositionists there are also communist fundamentalists who are incapable of freeing themselves from the grip of dogmatic ideas. Despite facts that everyone now knows and despite the present state of public opinion they do not want to admit what a monstrous price had to be paid for the doctrinaire behaviour and an unlimited faith in ideological dogmas and myths. They demand that the Party should again be made the backbone of the state and the manager of all activity in society, a commanding force. They declare reform of the political system to be a political plot directed against the people and they brand the democratization of the economy as a return to the pre-revolutionary system. The slogans of their campaign are revealing: they are against opportunists, revisionists, neo-Mensheviks, national communists and 'social traitors'.

That is a policy leading once again to the division of society into reds and whites and ultimately to civil disaster. No references to mistakes made in the course of *perestroika* can justify such a position.

Mistakes are inevitable in such a tremendous task as managing the transition of a huge, very complex, multinational country of 300 million inhabitants to a fundamentally different path of development. There are no saints in such an undertaking. The only thing that I can assert with a clear conscience is that throughout the six years I have never yielded to the temptation to retreat, to give up, to reject the chosen objective or to absolve myself of responsibility for the adopted cause and for moving it ahead. I did not make that mistake, the greatest possible one.

Now about the allegation that it was at the nineteenth Party Conference that the main mistake was made on the way of *perestroika*. No. The historic, crucial significance of the Conference consists precisely in the fact that it was then said and *demonstrated* before the whole world that we were not playing at democracy but were taking its principles seriously and intended to act in accordance with the laws it had established in the course of world development. The Conference really did spur on the rapid development of the democratic process in our country. By so doing it opened up more and more and revealed the *main point* of *perestroika*: that society has to develop, not on orders from above, not according to an already prescribed recipe, and not under the control of bodies exercising a monopoly over ideology and politics, but according to the natural logic of democratic advance, freely exercising its social and intellectual potential. It will move forward in a continuous quest on a pluralistic basis, a quest for appropriate political decisions needed to bring order into this historic process.

The nineteenth Party Conference put the process of reform in our society on the right track, and made it irreversible.

The democratization of society in our country would be doomed if it were not extended to relations between the nationalities and the rights of all peoples. But the process of reviving national self-awareness and self-determination, that had been started with the support and understanding of the initiators of *perestroika*, acquired an explosive, disruptive character. In a number of cases it was headed by people who were either politically inexperienced or simply irresponsible, embittered nationalists. But when events led to bloodshed it was, in their eyes, the 'centre' that was to blame because it had 'not taken precautions', 'not prevented', 'been too late', or, on the contrary, 'had no right to intervene'. In all these accusations there was only one true message: that the 'centre' should have supported somebody's side, and in fact 'my' side, against the other.

We recognized the Leninist principle of self-determination

in practice right up to secession, and we rejected the Stalinist unitarist conception of the state which was a fundamental distortion of Lenin's understanding of a Soviet federation, and we gave the republics the freedom to reorganize their Union on truly voluntary and equal federative principles. In reply the neo-internationalists − if you scratch them, just chauvinists − raised the cry: our great multinational state is collapsing, the 'indestructible friendship of the peoples' is being destroyed.

It really is a question of the fate of our country, of our native land, of our common home, of how we, our children and our grandchildren, are going to live. It is a problem on such a scale and of such importance that it takes precedence over the interests of particular parties, social groups and political and social movements. It was for that very reason that I was a determined supporter of a nationwide referendum. And despite, as it seemed, the very unfavourable conditions in the social and economic field and the growth of discontent due to the falling standard of living, the people manifested their good sense, their strong sense of responsibility, their patriotism in action. The majority voted in favour of maintaining the integrity of the state, which was a thousand years old and which had been created by the efforts and intellect, and by innumerable sacrifices, of many generations. They voted for the Union in which the fate of the people and millions of human lives were indissolubly interwoven. The referendum demonstrated people's self-respect in pride for the state that had more than once proved its ability to defend the independence and security of the peoples united within it and which was now asserting itself as the initiator and bastion of genuine peace and global stability. The referendum provided authoritative moral and political support for speeding up work on the Union treaty.

The public is coming to understand ever more clearly that,

having rejected one extreme – the unitarist type of state in which the republics were not given the opportunity to decide the problems they are now deciding as they are becoming sovereign states – we should not make the mistake of falling into the other extreme and turning the Union into something amorphous and ineffective. That would be a disaster no less than the one that the totalitarian unitary system led to. In the course of 1000 years in one case, of 200 to 300 in another and of 50 in the third case such realities had taken shape for the healthy growth of which was required a vital, real federation and not some loose community or association.

There is talk of the collapse of our state. But it is not the state that is collapsing. Having taken shape over the course of centuries, it is alive today and will continue to live. What is collapsing is its command structures, which sought to bring together the republics and people by direction from above and has come into contradiction with the demands of further development and with the aspirations of the peoples themselves. The present outburst of national and nationalist emotions is convincing evidence of how unsatisfactory and undesired the previous structure was and how dangerous were the diseases undermining the Union. It was precisely those that brought about a real prospect of the state collapsing. Could anyone really think seriously today, on the threshold of the twenty-first century, when a vast wave of democratization is sweeping across the world, that anybody would be capable of building or holding together a multinational state by compulsion?

Today a genuinely voluntary community of peoples is being put together and that will give unprecedented stability to our Union. As the relations laid down in the Union treaty become a reality our renewed Union will be filled with life and will consolidate itself. A new time will begin for it, a time of strengthening the voluntary and natural links between the peoples of our country.

We are creating a *modern* state and the criteria by which to judge its strength and greatness are very different from what they were. Today only a *democratic* state can be great. A modern state is not strong by virtue of its tight control over all aspects of life, nor of its command methods of rule, nor of the people's readiness to march in the direction handed down from above, but by virtue of democratic agreement, freedom, the spirit of liberty, the exercise of initiative and a high standard of living for its citizens. On the territory of practically a whole continent we are creating a new democratic area, political, economic and spiritual. We are creating a great democratic state which will not be condemned to be eternally trying to catch up with the advanced countries.

The conclusion of the Union treaty will make it possible at last to stem the destructive processes and make a decisive move towards the restoration of normal conditions of life and work.

We are on the eve of a crucial, great event in the history of our country. As a result of heated discussions, a tremendous amount of creative work that has brought together the opinions, concerns and interests of dozens of peoples, as a result of a difficult political battle, which only testifies to the grandiose nature of our cause, there is emerging a new, quite unprecedented state, a great power, built on new foundations of complete voluntariness and equality. And it will be a strong power, not by virtue of its military might and ability to inspire fear, as it did for a long time in the past, but primarily because of the social and economic health of its multimillion and multinational population living in conditions of democracy and economic and political freedom. Its vitality will derive its strength from the agreement and joint work and a reasonable and fair division of labour between all the nations and their sovereign state formations.

Such is one of the aims of *perestroika*, with implications for world history.

Life and time have arranged things in such a way that the overdue bills have to be paid by the present generation of leaders, at the centre, in the republics and locally. All the greater is the responsibility that falls on all of us to make sure that the great and truly historical cause of reuniting our nations once again should be crowned with complete success.

The euphoria of separatism and national extremism can be explained and to a certain extent understood at a stage when the contradictions of a unitarist totalitarian state, which were accumulating for a long time, have finally exploded.

But when we – through the Union treaty – create a market economy area, covering the entire country and becoming ever more involved in the world market, when the machinery of coordination between the sovereign republics begins to oper-ate, when we begin jointly to emerge from the crisis and people begin to enjoy the first material fruits of *perestroika*, cultivated thanks to their unity and inter-ethnic accord – then all those honest people (and most of them really are honest) who were carried away by the nationalist tendencies and did not come to their senses in time and did not stop their leaders, with their slogan: the worse it is for the Union the better it is for my nation – those people will not only be ashamed of themselves. They will see what a tremendous mistake they made when they did not join in a great integrational process on one sixth of the territory of our planet.

Perestroika could not be carried through in an international vacuum, especially not in a hostile external environment. That, it would seem, is clear to everybody. But when concrete steps were taken to end the confrontation with the West, which had long been quite pointless, extremely dangerous and impossibly costly, accusations came pouring down: that what imperialism had not obtained by force we were handing them on a platter, that we had lost the 'third world war', that we had handed over what had been won in the Patriotic war of 1941–1945, that we were insulting the memory of the millions sacrificed in that war, that we were betraying our friends and allies, that we had destroyed the socialist system, that we had struck a blow in the back of international communism, and so forth.

As a result, it was alleged, *perestroika* had weakened the foreign policy positions of our great state and we were dancing to someone else's tune, and so on. Let us go into this. The Soviet Union really did make desperate efforts to play the part of a 'super-power', but it succeeded in doing so only in one respect – the military. So our prestige was the prestige of military force, the prestige of the threat. Soviet troops were stationed in Eastern Europe and in Mongolia, our young men were dying in Afghanistan. At the same time the excessive military machine that had been created undermined our economy and condemned the non-military branches of the economy to appalling stagnation and the standard of living to decline. On top of that our military potential also began gradually to decline because of our increasing technical backwardness and excessive expenditure. In the end we could have found ourselves faced with the choice: either to bring the whole world into our gunsights or agree to fall behind in the military sense. We were a super-power with an inefficient economy and had become merely an appendage for the supply of raw materials to the more advanced countries, while our standard of living was far inferior to theirs. Is it patriotic for citizens anxious about their country's prestige to feel nostalgic for all that?

We put an end to the foreign policy that served the utopian aim of spreading communist ideas round the world, had led us into the dead end of the Cold War, inflicted on the people an intolerable burden of military expenditure, and dragged us into adventures like the one in Afghanistan. For the first time in many years and decades a foreign policy is being conducted that serves *our own national interests* and works to benefit our domestic development.

At the same time we have acquired unprecedentedly high authority internationally, but of a different kind – an authority based on trust, the authority of a foreign policy that is constructive, predictable, moral and free of adventurism. The liberation of mankind from the threat of a nuclear Armageddon has in fact increased our own country's security. A firm basis has been created for the further strengthening of the foreign policy positions of our state. Let us recall that great Russian minister of foreign affairs in the last century, Prince Gorchakov, who said: 'Russia is concentrating' when referring to the revival of her authority following the reforms of the 1860s and 1870s.

The Soviet Union remains and will remain a great power, without which world issues cannot be decided. But we have become a normal member of the world community and are merging on a basis of equality into the common stream of world civilization.

There is talk about the 'selling off' of our state with reference to the various contacts with other states, the stream of foreigners arriving in our country, and the increasing – although not rapidly enough – activity of foreign capital in the Soviet Union. But is patriotism really a matter of isolating one's country from world progress and from scientific, technical and cultural achievements? In that case even Peter the Great, who 'opened up a window to Europe', and made great use of the experience, knowledge and technical ability of the Europeans, was no patriot.

Today particularly, patriotism consists in moving our country forward more quickly to acquire the achievements of science and technology, the achievements of world civilization. That is exactly what we are doing and on that bridgehead we are also creating the prerequisites for the renewal, revival and strengthening of our great state.

A situation where the threat of a world war has disappeared has exposed the absurdity and great danger of super-militarization. The refusal to continue the Cold War and the arms race that has exhausted the country's resources and brought it to the brink of economic collapse, has had its effect on the army and all the branches of the economy that supplied it, on the military-industrial complex.

The people whose interests were affected, even if they under-stood the inevitability of the changes, especially those who decided to exploit the social and psychological consequences of returning our troops from foreign countries, the reduction in the numbers of personnel and armaments, and the conver-sion of the arms industry – those people opened up yet another front against *perestroika*.

They resorted to the most brazen demagogy: we had left the Army to the mercy of fate, undermined the main support for our state system, humiliated the generals and marshals, and so forth. They were and still are hitting the tenderest spots, touching not just on the material everyday side of the problem but also on the patriotic emotions and our people's traditional respect for military service. This unbridled dema-gogy, which embittered the military and evoked legitimate anger in Army circles and in the public generally, is being helped by those who – out of self-interest or nationalistic convictions – indulge in abuse of the Army and slander it, and who insult officers and soldiers in public, and by local authorities in some places who try to do them every kind of harm and worsen their conditions of life and service.

Thinking about all these by-products of the process of *perestroika*, of the turmoil which is in many ways inevitable in a time of revolutionary transition from one system to another, the following thought comes to mind.

The great misfortune for the old Russia, because of which the February Revolution came to nothing and the idea behind the October Revolution failed, was the fact that the millions of ordinary people were illiterate, which meant that they were cut off from political life. In deciding the country's fate they acted as a material force easily controlled with the aid of quite primitive means.

The misfortune for the Soviet Union was the fact that the people were given literacy in order to impose on them a ready-made programme of development, to stir up hatred of everything that was unlike that programme, to isolate the people from the outside world and from the advance of civilization. As a result the people became an instrument for manipulation by political adventurers for whom the whole purpose of life was unlimited power, the unquestioning subordination of people to their will, and total arbitrariness, contrary to moral standards and human rights.

The thought does not leave me that, had it not been for Stalin's *Thermidor* in the mid 1920s, which betrayed and trampled on the ideas of the Great Revolution – a revolution that was genuinely popular and for the people – it might still have been possible to direct the country along the path of democratic progress, revival and economic prosperity, to correct the mistakes and injustices committed in the course of the civil war, and to heal the spiritual wounds.

Alas, what happened was worse than might have been

expected although even then in both camps – the red and the white – some prophecies were made in this regard that were striking in their depth of vision. But I will not go into that here.

It is only now, in the course of the last few years, that we have had access to knowledge of the true state of humanity in the second half of the twentieth century, that we could look at ourselves through the eyes of outstanding thinkers and writers who have been driven out of their country but have remained her passionate patriots, that we have freed ourselves of fear and have begun to extricate ourselves from the grip of the dogmas and stereotypes of the Stalin period and return to our senses – it is only now that has begun to emerge the spiritual environment needed for a correct understanding of what our own country and its destiny really are. But we are still only at the beginning of this discovery of ourselves and certainly of digesting all that we have learnt and understood: I have in mind the majority of our citizens, including a considerable section of the intelligentsia.

The period of self-awareness and purification has been dragged out, and has in its turn introduced much that is negative and built new obstacles on the paths to common sense and agreement.

Even some genuinely great and original intellectual and artistic discoveries and achievements of the Soviet epoch which are recognized worldwide, are now being negated.

All this chaotic, turbulent and passionate movement, in which there is a great deal of sincerity and longing for better things for one's country, was something that our country had to go through. We had to pass through that so as to refresh our brains, to try and clear our consciences, to understand where we were, and to recognize reality. But, to use a Biblical metaphor, the stones have been thrown far apart. More than that, by projecting what used to be on to what is happening now, we have done a lot of harm to people, ideas and deeds associated with *perestroika*.

It is already time to gather the stones. This process began with the '9 plus 1' Declaration. At a moment of dangerous confrontation in the spring which had threatened to overrun all limits, the principal political forces managed to recognize their responsibility and to agree on how by their joint efforts they could extricate the country from the crisis. The '9 plus 1' agreement made it possible to defuse the situation. It played a salutary role and laid the foundation for a tendency towards reaching agreement and stabilization. Its sources are the people's instinct of self-preservation, their disgust with bickering, a natural aspiration to reach agreement in the cause of saving the country, and simply a sobering up after the shock of learning the truth which turned out to be so tragic. The possibility appeared of conducting political life within the framework of the law and the functioning of the legal institutions of democracy created as a result of *perestroika*, and of excluding the solution of problems by screaming mobs and cries of 'Down with . . .' Tendencies are becoming stronger in society to calm down and to resolve problems in a business-like way in accordance with the principles that lie at the basis of *perestroika*. Constructive ideas have been put forward concerning the movement ahead. Party programmes and draft constitutions have been written and new legislation is being drawn up.

Innumerable plans for 'saving the country' have been published in newspapers and magazines. They include many interesting ideas and good intentions. However, a feature common to most of them is the tendency to want to impose on the country yet another ideal model which, from the point of view of each author, is the best and most effective. It is essentially a question of forcing society into a ready-made mould in which everything is laid down according to functions and times and which, if everyone performs as prescribed, will guarantee the desired result. We have already been through that sort of thing.

But we must not allow all this to be taken, not as part of a debate and as a natural and normal way of seeking for the truth, but as a confrontation between the 'reds and whites', the 'blues and the blacks', the revisionists and the traitors, the enemies of the people and the people's 'true friends'. That would mean returning to the 1930s. People have various opinions and different potential. There will be conflicts and different approaches to questions. That is natural and therein lies a source of movement. The suppression of independent thought and of dissenting opinions is a way to snuff out society.

At the same time we are witnesses to the emergence of all kinds of parties, movements, unions, associations, clubs and so forth. What is positive here is that it testifies to the reactivation of the public's awareness, of an awakened collective intellect and of the growth of people's eagerness to take part in political life which cannot henceforth be the affair of only the leaders and authorities. But this multiplicity of groupings also reflects the strivings of various sections of society to stand up for their own special interests and their specific needs in opposition to other people's. Such conflicts – and we witness open hostility between representatives of various interests – are dangerous. Here you have an explosive mixture building up, here is the source of destabilization and the threat of a breakdown of the positive tendencies.

That is why we now need clear guidelines to lead us towards agreement and unity around national and all-Union tasks – immediate and long-term, outside the scope of which specific goals cannot be achieved. We need to gather up all our strength in support of the positions and principles for transforming the country that have already been worked out: a mixed economy, various forms of property, democratic institutions, a strict separation of powers and a new Federative Union. In a word, the democratic reform of society calculated to lead the country onwards to the most advanced frontiers of modern civilization through the integration of the Soviet Union with the world community.

All this taken together forms the common national idea which is so necessary for us if we are to have popular accord and a peaceful advance along the path of *perestroika*.

The Novo-Ogarevo process, which has led to the Union treaty, has within it a real safety mechanism for the country's self-preservation. We must hold on to that, constantly keeping before us the key objectives of *perestroika*: political freedom, economic freedom and intellectual freedom. We must stand firm and hold on . . . and make sure that we do not open the way for the neo-Stalinists, the retrograde types, nor for the adventurists and ultra-radicals, and so keep *perestroika* on a peaceful course. Otherwise everything will go back to the old ways.

Such a change of course as has fallen to the lot of our generation and such reforms, involving change in the very way of life, affecting property, productive relations and man's position in society, have nowhere and never in the whole of world history been painless or easy. Many countries have gone through critical stages but have come through all right and have acquired fresh strength and moved on further.

In the course of our centuries-long history there have more than once been critical periods when Russia had to be revived, and it was always a painful leap, since she did not know how to take the paths of reformist evolution: the old relationships resisted to the end, to the last ditch, one might say. And there was no shortage of gloomy prophecies or of panic-stricken declarations about an inevitable catastrophe. Nevertheless the country usually came out of these difficult periods stronger and sturdier. That is how it will be with the Soviet Union.

But the same historical experience teaches that the beneficial consequences of reform are not apparent immediately and that the country has to pay a price of pain and suffering for them. So we are now paying that price for our liberation from the political, economic and spiritual shackles and for advancing towards a new, stronger and more vigorous state.

But we have to make ourselves understand more quickly that any society or state can develop normally only if there exists a strong executive authority based on popular support. That requires the agreement of the main political forces and their readiness to act together in the interests of the nation as a whole. And let them not be frightened by problems: if there are none it means that the society has come to a halt and will perish. If there is movement there will be problems.

Alongside the bitter weeds and the signs of disappointment and cynicism – which is the price we have to pay for breaking down the false stereotypes imposed for decades – there are other aspects from which we can derive hope and optimism: the growth in society of the civic spirit, the Soviet people's growing awareness of their rights and their readiness to defend those rights, their political activism, and an increase in political sense and responsibility. A new generation, rid of ideological blinkers, capable of thinking critically and independent in its judgements, is being born and we can entrust the country's future to it.

The most important thing is not to give in now at the most critical crossing point, not to stop and not to seek salvation in the past – that would be the greatest, irreparable mistake.

It would be suicidal if we were again this time, as in the 1950s and 1960s, to take fright and stop half-way. Then we shall slide back.

It is right to say that everything has to mature. But our time is now running out. There is no need to panic or get confused. We need to keep a cool head and self-control and have courage. But also needed are clear thinking and a keen reaction to the conflicting processes. And, of course, faith in the cause we have initiated.

For that it is important not to lose our bearings, remain devoted to the socialist perspective and to advance, in spite of difficulties and mistakes, along the path of radical democratic transformations and the creation of normal social conditions. At the same time we must remember that at the very centre of *perestroika* is the most reliable social safety net. *Perestroika* will provide people with the opportunity to work and display initiative, will generate powerful incentives for good work. There lies the main basis for real social protection of the individual.

The situation is such that practical moves should not be delayed. Everything should be done in such a way that the fruits of what was started six years ago should be visible to the people as quickly as possible – on the shop shelves, on the streets, in public transport, in daily life and in the workplace.

We can even in the near future achieve the initial results and gather the necessary momentum to satisfy the most pressing needs of the population. The longer term harvest will probably be richer. But we are hopeful that everything we are doing will enable people to feel fairly soon that their expectations are justified.